C-3807

CAREER EXAMINATIO[

THIS IS YOUR **PASSBOOK®** FOR ...

STATION AGENT

NATIONAL LEARNING CORPORATION®

passbooks.com

COPYRIGHT NOTICE

NLC®

National Learning Corporation

212 Michael Drive, Syosset, NY 11791
(516) 921-8888 • www.passbooks.com
E-mail: info@passbooks.com

PUBLISHED IN THE UNITED STATES OF AMERICA

PASSBOOK® SERIES

THE *PASSBOOK® SERIES* has been created to prepare applicants and candidates for the ultimate academic battlefield – the examination room.

At some time in our lives, each and every one of us may be required to take an examination – for validation, matriculation, admission, qualification, registration, certification, or licensure.

Based on the assumption that every applicant or candidate has met the basic formal educational standards, has taken the required number of courses, and read the necessary texts, the *PASSBOOK® SERIES* furnishes the one special preparation which may assure passing with confidence, instead of failing with insecurity. Examination questions – together with answers – are furnished as the basic vehicle for study so that the mysteries of the examination and its compounding difficulties may be eliminated or diminished by a sure method.

This book is meant to help you pass your examination provided that you qualify and are serious in your objective.

The entire field is reviewed through the huge store of content information which is succinctly presented through a provocative and challenging approach – the question-and-answer method.

A climate of success is established by furnishing the correct answers at the end of each test.

You soon learn to recognize types of questions, forms of questions, and patterns of questioning. You may even begin to anticipate expected outcomes.

You perceive that many questions are repeated or adapted so that you can gain acute insights, which may enable you to score many sure points.

You learn how to confront new questions, or types of questions, and to attack them confidently and work out the correct answers.

You note objectives and emphases, and recognize pitfalls and dangers, so that you may make positive educational adjustments.

Moreover, you are kept fully informed in relation to new concepts, methods, practices, and directions in the field.

You discover that you arre actually taking the examination all the time: you are preparing for the examination by "taking" an examination, not by reading extraneous and/or supererogatory textbooks.

In short, this PASSBOOK®, used directedly, should be an important factor in helping you to pass your test.

STATION AGENT

DUTIES

Station Agents, under general supervision, provide direct customer service; are required to listen to, understand and give customers solutions to their concerns, problems and complaints; provide customers with travel and transit system-related information and services, and help customers with purchase and use of fare cards; perform maintenance on station equipment, observe and report on overall station conditions; sell fare cards to customers; and perform such other duties as the transit authority is authorized by law to prescribe in its regulations.

THE TEST

The multiple-choice test may include questions on resolving customers' concerns, problems or complaints; interpreting timetables, subway maps and other printed material; understanding subway operating procedures; following procedures in the event of emergencies or unusual occurrences; job-related arithmetic; points of interest in the City; and other related areas.

HOW TO TAKE A TEST

I. YOU MUST PASS AN EXAMINATION

A. WHAT EVERY CANDIDATE SHOULD KNOW

Examination applicants often ask us for help in preparing for the written test. What can I study in advance? What kinds of questions will be asked? How will the test be given? How will the papers be graded?

As an applicant for a civil service examination, you may be wondering about some of these things. Our purpose here is to suggest effective methods of advance study and to describe civil service examinations.

Your chances for success on this examination can be increased if you know how to prepare. Those "pre-examination jitters" can be reduced if you know what to expect. You can even experience an adventure in good citizenship if you know why civil service exams are given.

B. WHY ARE CIVIL SERVICE EXAMINATIONS GIVEN?

Civil service examinations are important to you in two ways. As a citizen, you want public jobs filled by employees who know how to do their work. As a job seeker, you want a fair chance to compete for that job on an equal footing with other candidates. The best-known means of accomplishing this two-fold goal is the competitive examination.

Exams are widely publicized throughout the nation. They may be administered for jobs in federal, state, city, municipal, town or village governments or agencies.

Any citizen may apply, with some limitations, such as the age or residence of applicants. Your experience and education may be reviewed to see whether you meet the requirements for the particular examination. When these requirements exist, they are reasonable and applied consistently to all applicants. Thus, a competitive examination may cause you some uneasiness now, but it is your privilege and safeguard.

C. HOW ARE CIVIL SERVICE EXAMS DEVELOPED?

Examinations are carefully written by trained technicians who are specialists in the field known as "psychological measurement," in consultation with recognized authorities in the field of work that the test will cover. These experts recommend the subject matter areas or skills to be tested; only those knowledges or skills important to your success on the job are included. The most reliable books and source materials available are used as references. Together, the experts and technicians judge the difficulty level of the questions.

Test technicians know how to phrase questions so that the problem is clearly stated. Their ethics do not permit "trick" or "catch" questions. Questions may have been tried out on sample groups, or subjected to statistical analysis, to determine their usefulness.

Written tests are often used in combination with performance tests, ratings of training and experience, and oral interviews. All of these measures combine to form the best-known means of finding the right person for the right job.

II. HOW TO PASS THE WRITTEN TEST

A. NATURE OF THE EXAMINATION

To prepare intelligently for civil service examinations, you should know how they differ from school examinations you have taken. In school you were assigned certain definite pages to read or subjects to cover. The examination questions were quite detailed and usually emphasized memory. Civil service exams, on the other hand, try to discover your present ability to perform the duties of a position, plus your potentiality to learn these duties. In other words, a civil service exam attempts to predict how successful you will be. Questions cover such a broad area that they cannot be as minute and detailed as school exam questions.

In the public service similar kinds of work, or positions, are grouped together in one "class." This process is known as *position-classification*. All the positions in a class are paid according to the salary range for that class. One class title covers all of these positions, and they are all tested by the same examination.

B. FOUR BASIC STEPS

1) Study the announcement

How, then, can you know what subjects to study? Our best answer is: "Learn as much as possible about the class of positions for which you've applied." The exam will test the knowledge, skills and abilities needed to do the work.

Your most valuable source of information about the position you want is the official exam announcement. This announcement lists the training and experience qualifications. Check these standards and apply only if you come reasonably close to meeting them.

The brief description of the position in the examination announcement offers some clues to the subjects which will be tested. Think about the job itself. Review the duties in your mind. Can you perform them, or are there some in which you are rusty? Fill in the blank spots in your preparation.

Many jurisdictions preview the written test in the exam announcement by including a section called "Knowledge and Abilities Required," "Scope of the Examination," or some similar heading. Here you will find out specifically what fields will be tested.

2) Review your own background

Once you learn in general what the position is all about, and what you need to know to do the work, ask yourself which subjects you already know fairly well and which need improvement. You may wonder whether to concentrate on improving your strong areas or on building some background in your fields of weakness. When the announcement has specified "some knowledge" or "considerable knowledge," or has used adjectives like "beginning principles of..." or "advanced ... methods," you can get a clue as to the number and difficulty of questions to be asked in any given field. More questions, and hence broader coverage, would be included for those subjects which are more important in the work. Now weigh your strengths and weaknesses against the job requirements and prepare accordingly.

3) Determine the level of the position

Another way to tell how intensively you should prepare is to understand the level of the job for which you are applying. Is it the entering level? In other words, is this the position in which beginners in a field of work are hired? Or is it an intermediate or advanced level? Sometimes this is indicated by such words as "Junior" or "Senior" in the class title. Other jurisdictions use Roman numerals to designate the level – Clerk I, Clerk II, for example. The word "Supervisor" sometimes appears in the title. If the level is not indicated by the title, check the description of duties. Will you be working under very close supervision, or will you have responsibility for independent decisions in this work?

4) Choose appropriate study materials

Now that you know the subjects to be examined and the relative amount of each subject to be covered, you can choose suitable study materials. For beginning level jobs, or even advanced ones, if you have a pronounced weakness in some aspect of your training, read a modern, standard textbook in that field. Be sure it is up to date and has general coverage. Such books are normally available at your library, and the librarian will be glad to help you locate one. For entry-level positions, questions of appropriate difficulty are chosen – neither highly advanced questions, nor those too simple. Such questions require careful thought but not advanced training.

If the position for which you are applying is technical or advanced, you will read more advanced, specialized material. If you are already familiar with the basic principles of your field, elementary textbooks would waste your time. Concentrate on advanced textbooks and technical periodicals. Think through the concepts and review difficult problems in your field.

These are all general sources. You can get more ideas on your own initiative, following these leads. For example, training manuals and publications of the government agency which employs workers in your field can be useful, particularly for technical and professional positions. A letter or visit to the government department involved may result in more specific study suggestions, and certainly will provide you with a more definite idea of the exact nature of the position you are seeking.

III. KINDS OF TESTS

Tests are used for purposes other than measuring knowledge and ability to perform specified duties. For some positions, it is equally important to test ability to make adjustments to new situations or to profit from training. In others, basic mental abilities not dependent on information are essential. Questions which test these things may not appear as pertinent to the duties of the position as those which test for knowledge and information. Yet they are often highly important parts of a fair examination. For very general questions, it is almost impossible to help you direct your study efforts. What we can do is to point out some of the more common of these general abilities needed in public service positions and describe some typical questions.

1) General information

Broad, general information has been found useful for predicting job success in some kinds of work. This is tested in a variety of ways, from vocabulary lists to questions about current events. Basic background in some field of work, such as sociology or economics, may be sampled in a group of questions. Often these are principles which have become familiar to most persons through exposure rather than through formal training. It is difficult to advise you how to study for these questions; being alert to the world around you is our best suggestion.

2) Verbal ability

An example of an ability needed in many positions is verbal or language ability. Verbal ability is, in brief, the ability to use and understand words. Vocabulary and grammar tests are typical measures of this ability. Reading comprehension or paragraph interpretation questions are common in many kinds of civil service tests. You are given a paragraph of written material and asked to find its central meaning.

3) Numerical ability

Number skills can be tested by the familiar arithmetic problem, by checking paired lists of numbers to see which are alike and which are different, or by interpreting charts and graphs. In the latter test, a graph may be printed in the test booklet which you are asked to use as the basis for answering questions.

4) Observation

A popular test for law-enforcement positions is the observation test. A picture is shown to you for several minutes, then taken away. Questions about the picture test your ability to observe both details and larger elements.

5) Following directions

In many positions in the public service, the employee must be able to carry out written instructions dependably and accurately. You may be given a chart with several columns, each column listing a variety of information. The questions require you to carry out directions involving the information given in the chart.

6) Skills and aptitudes

Performance tests effectively measure some manual skills and aptitudes. When the skill is one in which you are trained, such as typing or shorthand, you can practice. These tests are often very much like those given in business school or high school courses. For many of the other skills and aptitudes, however, no short-time preparation can be made. Skills and abilities natural to you or that you have developed throughout your lifetime are being tested.

Many of the general questions just described provide all the data needed to answer the questions and ask you to use your reasoning ability to find the answers. Your best preparation for these tests, as well as for tests of facts and ideas, is to be at your physical and mental best. You, no doubt, have your own methods of getting into an exam-taking mood and keeping “in shape.” The next section lists some ideas on this subject.

IV. KINDS OF QUESTIONS

Only rarely is the “essay” question, which you answer in narrative form, used in civil service tests. Civil service tests are usually of the short-answer type. Full instructions for answering these questions will be given to you at the examination. But in case this is your first experience with short-answer questions and separate answer sheets, here is what you need to know:

1) Multiple-choice Questions

Most popular of the short-answer questions is the "multiple choice" or "best answer" question. It can be used, for example, to test for factual knowledge, ability to solve problems or judgment in meeting situations found at work.

A multiple-choice question is normally one of three types—

- It can begin with an incomplete statement followed by several possible endings. You are to find the one ending which *best* completes the statement, although some of the others may not be entirely wrong.
- It can also be a complete statement in the form of a question which is answered by choosing one of the statements listed.
- It can be in the form of a problem – again you select the best answer.

Here is an example of a multiple-choice question with a discussion which should give you some clues as to the method for choosing the right answer:

When an employee has a complaint about his assignment, the action which will *best* help him overcome his difficulty is to

A. discuss his difficulty with his coworkers
B. take the problem to the head of the organization
C. take the problem to the person who gave him the assignment
D. say nothing to anyone about his complaint

In answering this question, you should study each of the choices to find which is best. Consider choice "A" – Certainly an employee may discuss his complaint with fellow employees, but no change or improvement can result, and the complaint remains unresolved. Choice "B" is a poor choice since the head of the organization probably does not know what assignment you have been given, and taking your problem to him is known as "going over the head" of the supervisor. The supervisor, or person who made the assignment, is the person who can clarify it or correct any injustice. Choice "C" is, therefore, correct. To say nothing, as in choice "D," is unwise. Supervisors have and interest in knowing the problems employees are facing, and the employee is seeking a solution to his problem.

2) True/False Questions

The "true/false" or "right/wrong" form of question is sometimes used. Here a complete statement is given. Your job is to decide whether the statement is right or wrong.

SAMPLE: A roaming cell-phone call to a nearby city costs less than a non-roaming call to a distant city.

This statement is wrong, or false, since roaming calls are more expensive.

This is not a complete list of all possible question forms, although most of the others are variations of these common types. You will always get complete directions for answering questions. Be sure you understand *how* to mark your answers – ask questions until you do.

V. RECORDING YOUR ANSWERS

Computer terminals are used more and more today for many different kinds of exams.

For an examination with very few applicants, you may be told to record your answers in the test booklet itself. Separate answer sheets are much more common. If this separate answer sheet is to be scored by machine – and this is often the case – it is highly important that you mark your answers correctly in order to get credit.

An electronic scoring machine is often used in civil service offices because of the speed with which papers can be scored. Machine-scored answer sheets must be marked with a pencil, which will be given to you. This pencil has a high graphite content which responds to the electronic scoring machine. As a matter of fact, stray dots may register as answers, so do not let your pencil rest on the answer sheet while you are pondering the correct answer. Also, if your pencil lead breaks or is otherwise defective, ask for another.

Since the answer sheet will be dropped in a slot in the scoring machine, be careful not to bend the corners or get the paper crumpled.

The answer sheet normally has five vertical columns of numbers, with 30 numbers to a column. These numbers correspond to the question numbers in your test booklet. After each number, going across the page are four or five pairs of dotted lines. These short dotted lines have small letters or numbers above them. The first two pairs may also have a "T" or "F" above the letters. This indicates that the first two pairs only are to be used if the questions are of the true-false type. If the questions are multiple choice, disregard the "T" and "F" and pay attention only to the small letters or numbers.

Answer your questions in the manner of the sample that follows:

32. The largest city in the United States is
    A. Washington, D.C.
    B. New York City
    C. Chicago
    D. Detroit
    E. San Francisco

1) Choose the answer you think is best. (New York City is the largest, so "B" is correct.)
2) Find the row of dotted lines numbered the same as the question you are answering. (Find row number 32)
3) Find the pair of dotted lines corresponding to the answer. (Find the pair of lines under the mark "B.")
4) Make a solid black mark between the dotted lines.

VI. BEFORE THE TEST

Common sense will help you find procedures to follow to get ready for an examination. Too many of us, however, overlook these sensible measures. Indeed, nervousness and fatigue have been found to be the most serious reasons why applicants fail to do their best on civil service tests. Here is a list of reminders:

- Begin your preparation early – Don't wait until the last minute to go scurrying around for books and materials or to find out what the position is all about.
- Prepare continuously – An hour a night for a week is better than an all-night cram session. This has been definitely established. What is more, a night a week for a month will return better dividends than crowding your study into a shorter period of time.
- Locate the place of the exam – You have been sent a notice telling you when and where to report for the examination. If the location is in a different town or otherwise unfamiliar to you, it would be well to inquire the best route and learn something about the building.
- Relax the night before the test – Allow your mind to rest. Do not study at all that night. Plan some mild recreation or diversion; then go to bed early and get a good night's sleep.
- Get up early enough to make a leisurely trip to the place for the test – This way unforeseen events, traffic snarls, unfamiliar buildings, etc. will not upset you.
- Dress comfortably – A written test is not a fashion show. You will be known by number and not by name, so wear something comfortable.
- Leave excess paraphernalia at home – Shopping bags and odd bundles will get in your way. You need bring only the items mentioned in the official notice you received; usually everything you need is provided. Do not bring reference books to the exam. They will only confuse those last minutes and be taken away from you when in the test room.
- Arrive somewhat ahead of time – If because of transportation schedules you must get there very early, bring a newspaper or magazine to take your mind off yourself while waiting.
- Locate the examination room – When you have found the proper room, you will be directed to the seat or part of the room where you will sit. Sometimes you are given a sheet of instructions to read while you are waiting. Do not fill out any forms until you are told to do so; just read them and be prepared.
- Relax and prepare to listen to the instructions
- If you have any physical problem that may keep you from doing your best, be sure to tell the test administrator. If you are sick or in poor health, you really cannot do your best on the exam. You can come back and take the test some other time.

VII. AT THE TEST

The day of the test is here and you have the test booklet in your hand. The temptation to get going is very strong. Caution! There is more to success than knowing the right answers. You must know how to identify your papers and understand variations in the type of short-answer question used in this particular examination. Follow these suggestions for maximum results from your efforts:

1) Cooperate with the monitor

The test administrator has a duty to create a situation in which you can be as much at ease as possible. He will give instructions, tell you when to begin, check to see that you are marking your answer sheet correctly, and so on. He is not there to guard you, although he will see that your competitors do not take unfair advantage. He wants to help you do your best.

2) Listen to all instructions

Don't jump the gun! Wait until you understand all directions. In most civil service tests you get more time than you need to answer the questions. So don't be in a hurry. Read each word of instructions until you clearly understand the meaning. Study the examples, listen to all announcements and follow directions. Ask questions if you do not understand what to do.

3) Identify your papers

Civil service exams are usually identified by number only. You will be assigned a number; you must not put your name on your test papers. Be sure to copy your number correctly. Since more than one exam may be given, copy your exact examination title.

4) Plan your time

Unless you are told that a test is a "speed" or "rate of work" test, speed itself is usually not important. Time enough to answer all the questions will be provided, but this does not mean that you have all day. An overall time limit has been set. Divide the total time (in minutes) by the number of questions to determine the approximate time you have for each question.

5) Do not linger over difficult questions

If you come across a difficult question, mark it with a paper clip (useful to have along) and come back to it when you have been through the booklet. One caution if you do this – be sure to skip a number on your answer sheet as well. Check often to be sure that you have not lost your place and that you are marking in the row numbered the same as the question you are answering.

6) Read the questions

Be sure you know what the question asks! Many capable people are unsuccessful because they failed to *read* the questions correctly.

7) Answer all questions

Unless you have been instructed that a penalty will be deducted for incorrect answers, it is better to guess than to omit a question.

8) Speed tests

It is often better NOT to guess on speed tests. It has been found that on timed tests people are tempted to spend the last few seconds before time is called in marking answers at random – without even reading them – in the hope of picking up a few extra points. To discourage this practice, the instructions may warn you that your score will be "corrected" for guessing. That is, a penalty will be applied. The incorrect answers will be deducted from the correct ones, or some other penalty formula will be used.

9) Review your answers

If you finish before time is called, go back to the questions you guessed or omitted to give them further thought. Review other answers if you have time.

10) Return your test materials

If you are ready to leave before others have finished or time is called, take ALL your materials to the monitor and leave quietly. Never take any test material with you. The monitor can discover whose papers are not complete, and taking a test booklet may be grounds for disqualification.

VIII. EXAMINATION TECHNIQUES

1) Read the general instructions carefully. These are usually printed on the first page of the exam booklet. As a rule, these instructions refer to the timing of the examination; the fact that you should not start work until the signal and must stop work at a signal, etc. If there are any *special* instructions, such as a choice of questions to be answered, make sure that you note this instruction carefully.

2) When you are ready to start work on the examination, that is as soon as the signal has been given, read the instructions to each question booklet, underline any key words or phrases, such as *least*, *best*, *outline*, *describe* and the like. In this way you will tend to answer as requested rather than discover on reviewing your paper that you *listed without describing*, that you selected the *worst* choice rather than the *best* choice, etc.

3) If the examination is of the objective or multiple-choice type – that is, each question will also give a series of possible answers: A, B, C or D, and you are called upon to select the best answer and write the letter next to that answer on your answer paper – it is advisable to start answering each question in turn. There may be anywhere from 50 to 100 such questions in the three or four hours allotted and you can see how much time would be taken if you read through all the questions before beginning to answer any. Furthermore, if you come across a question or group of questions which you know would be difficult to answer, it would undoubtedly affect your handling of all the other questions.

4) If the examination is of the essay type and contains but a few questions, it is a moot point as to whether you should read all the questions before starting to answer any one. Of course, if you are given a choice – say five out of seven and the like – then it is essential to read all the questions so you can eliminate the two that are most difficult. If, however, you are asked to answer all the questions, there may be danger in trying to answer the easiest one first because you may find that you will spend too much time on it. The best technique is to answer the first question, then proceed to the second, etc.

5) Time your answers. Before the exam begins, write down the time it started, then add the time allowed for the examination and write down the time it must be completed, then divide the time available somewhat as follows:

- If 3-1/2 hours are allowed, that would be 210 minutes. If you have 80 objective-type questions, that would be an average of 2-1/2 minutes per question. Allow yourself no more than 2 minutes per question, or a total of 160 minutes, which will permit about 50 minutes to review.
- If for the time allotment of 210 minutes there are 7 essay questions to answer, that would average about 30 minutes a question. Give yourself only 25 minutes per question so that you have about 35 minutes to review.

6) The most important instruction is to *read each question* and make sure you know what is wanted. The second most important instruction is to *time yourself properly* so that you answer every question. The third most important instruction is to *answer every question*. Guess if you have to but include something for each question. Remember that you will receive no credit for a blank and will probably receive some credit if you write something in answer to an essay question. If you guess a letter – say "B" for a multiple-choice question – you may have guessed right. If you leave a blank as an answer to a multiple-choice question, the examiners may respect your feelings but it will not add a point to your score. Some exams may penalize you for wrong answers, so in such cases *only*, you may not want to guess unless you have some basis for your answer.

7) Suggestions
   a. Objective-type questions
      1. Examine the question booklet for proper sequence of pages and questions
      2. Read all instructions carefully
      3. Skip any question which seems too difficult; return to it after all other questions have been answered
      4. Apportion your time properly; do not spend too much time on any single question or group of questions
      5. Note and underline key words – *all, most, fewest, least, best, worst, same, opposite,* etc.
      6. Pay particular attention to negatives
      7. Note unusual option, e.g., unduly long, short, complex, different or similar in content to the body of the question
      8. Observe the use of "hedging" words – *probably, may, most likely,* etc.
      9. Make sure that your answer is put next to the same number as the question
      10. Do not second-guess unless you have good reason to believe the second answer is definitely more correct
      11. Cross out original answer if you decide another answer is more accurate; do not erase until you are ready to hand your paper in
      12. Answer all questions; guess unless instructed otherwise
      13. Leave time for review

   b. Essay questions
      1. Read each question carefully
      2. Determine exactly what is wanted. Underline key words or phrases.
      3. Decide on outline or paragraph answer

4. Include many different points and elements unless asked to develop any one or two points or elements
5. Show impartiality by giving pros and cons unless directed to select one side only
6. Make and write down any assumptions you find necessary to answer the questions
7. Watch your English, grammar, punctuation and choice of words
8. Time your answers; don't crowd material

8) Answering the essay question

Most essay questions can be answered by framing the specific response around several key words or ideas. Here are a few such key words or ideas:

M's: manpower, materials, methods, money, management
P's: purpose, program, policy, plan, procedure, practice, problems, pitfalls, personnel, public relations

a. Six basic steps in handling problems:
   1. Preliminary plan and background development
   2. Collect information, data and facts
   3. Analyze and interpret information, data and facts
   4. Analyze and develop solutions as well as make recommendations
   5. Prepare report and sell recommendations
   6. Install recommendations and follow up effectiveness

b. Pitfalls to avoid
   1. *Taking things for granted* – A statement of the situation does not necessarily imply that each of the elements is necessarily true; for example, a complaint may be invalid and biased so that all that can be taken for granted is that a complaint has been registered
   2. *Considering only one side of a situation* – Wherever possible, indicate several alternatives and then point out the reasons you selected the best one
   3. *Failing to indicate follow up* – Whenever your answer indicates action on your part, make certain that you will take proper follow-up action to see how successful your recommendations, procedures or actions turn out to be
   4. *Taking too long in answering any single question* – Remember to time your answers properly

IX. AFTER THE TEST

Scoring procedures differ in detail among civil service jurisdictions although the general principles are the same. Whether the papers are hand-scored or graded by machine we have described, they are nearly always graded by number. That is, the person who marks the paper knows only the number – never the name – of the applicant. Not until all the papers have been graded will they be matched with names. If other tests, such as training and experience or oral interview ratings have been given, scores will be combined. Different parts of the examination usually have different weights. For example, the written test might count 60 percent of the final grade, and a rating of training and experience 40 percent. In many jurisdictions, veterans will have a certain number of points added to their grades.

After the final grade has been determined, the names are placed in grade order and an eligible list is established. There are various methods for resolving ties between those who get the same final grade – probably the most common is to place first the name of the person whose application was received first. Job offers are made from the eligible list in the order the names appear on it. You will be notified of your grade and your rank as soon as all these computations have been made. This will be done as rapidly as possible.

People who are found to meet the requirements in the announcement are called "eligibles." Their names are put on a list of eligible candidates. An eligible's chances of getting a job depend on how high he stands on this list and how fast agencies are filling jobs from the list.

When a job is to be filled from a list of eligibles, the agency asks for the names of people on the list of eligibles for that job. When the civil service commission receives this request, it sends to the agency the names of the three people highest on this list. Or, if the job to be filled has specialized requirements, the office sends the agency the names of the top three persons who meet these requirements from the general list.

The appointing officer makes a choice from among the three people whose names were sent to him. If the selected person accepts the appointment, the names of the others are put back on the list to be considered for future openings.

That is the rule in hiring from all kinds of eligible lists, whether they are for typist, carpenter, chemist, or something else. For every vacancy, the appointing officer has his choice of any one of the top three eligibles on the list. This explains why the person whose name is on top of the list sometimes does not get an appointment when some of the persons lower on the list do. If the appointing officer chooses the second or third eligible, the No. 1 eligible does not get a job at once, but stays on the list until he is appointed or the list is terminated.

X. HOW TO PASS THE INTERVIEW TEST

The examination for which you applied requires an oral interview test. You have already taken the written test and you are now being called for the interview test – the final part of the formal examination.

You may think that it is not possible to prepare for an interview test and that there are no procedures to follow during an interview. Our purpose is to point out some things you can do in advance that will help you and some good rules to follow and pitfalls to avoid while you are being interviewed.

What is an interview supposed to test?

The written examination is designed to test the technical knowledge and competence of the candidate; the oral is designed to evaluate intangible qualities, not readily measured otherwise, and to establish a list showing the relative fitness of each candidate – as measured against his competitors – for the position sought. Scoring is not on the basis of "right" and "wrong," but on a sliding scale of values ranging from "not passable" to "outstanding." As a matter of fact, it is possible to achieve a relatively low score without a single "incorrect" answer because of evident weakness in the qualities being measured.

Occasionally, an examination may consist entirely of an oral test – either an individual or a group oral. In such cases, information is sought concerning the technical knowledges and abilities of the candidate, since there has been no written examination for this purpose. More commonly, however, an oral test is used to supplement a written examination.

Who conducts interviews?

The composition of oral boards varies among different jurisdictions. In nearly all, a representative of the personnel department serves as chairman. One of the members of the board may be a representative of the department in which the candidate would work. In some cases, "outside experts" are used, and, frequently, a businessman or some other representative of the general public is asked to serve. Labor and management or other special groups may be represented. The aim is to secure the services of experts in the appropriate field.

However the board is composed, it is a good idea (and not at all improper or unethical) to ascertain in advance of the interview who the members are and what groups they represent. When you are introduced to them, you will have some idea of their backgrounds and interests, and at least you will not stutter and stammer over their names.

What should be done before the interview?

While knowledge about the board members is useful and takes some of the surprise element out of the interview, there is other preparation which is more substantive. It *is* possible to prepare for an oral interview – in several ways:

1) Keep a copy of your application and review it carefully before the interview

This may be the only document before the oral board, and the starting point of the interview. Know what education and experience you have listed there, and the sequence and dates of all of it. Sometimes the board will ask you to review the highlights of your experience for them; you should not have to hem and haw doing it.

2) Study the class specification and the examination announcement

Usually, the oral board has one or both of these to guide them. The qualities, characteristics or knowledges required by the position sought are stated in these documents. They offer valuable clues as to the nature of the oral interview. For example, if the job involves supervisory responsibilities, the announcement will usually indicate that knowledge of modern supervisory methods and the qualifications of the candidate as a supervisor will be tested. If so, you can expect such questions, frequently in the form of a hypothetical situation which you are expected to solve. NEVER go into an oral without knowledge of the duties and responsibilities of the job you seek.

3) Think through each qualification required

Try to visualize the kind of questions you would ask if you were a board member. How well could you answer them? Try especially to appraise your own knowledge and background in each area, *measured against the job sought*, and identify any areas in which you are weak. Be critical and realistic – do not flatter yourself.

4) Do some general reading in areas in which you feel you may be weak

For example, if the job involves supervision and your past experience has NOT, some general reading in supervisory methods and practices, particularly in the field of human relations, might be useful. Do NOT study agency procedures or detailed manuals. The oral board will be testing your understanding and capacity, not your memory.

5) Get a good night's sleep and watch your general health and mental attitude

You will want a clear head at the interview. Take care of a cold or any other minor ailment, and of course, no hangovers.

What should be done on the day of the interview?

Now comes the day of the interview itself. Give yourself plenty of time to get there. Plan to arrive somewhat ahead of the scheduled time, particularly if your appointment is in the fore part of the day. If a previous candidate fails to appear, the board might be ready for you a bit early. By early afternoon an oral board is almost invariably behind schedule if there are many candidates, and you may have to wait. Take along a book or magazine to read, or your application to review, but leave any extraneous material in the waiting room when you go in for your interview. In any event, relax and compose yourself.

The matter of dress is important. The board is forming impressions about you – from your experience, your manners, your attitude, and your appearance. Give your personal appearance careful attention. Dress your best, but not your flashiest. Choose conservative, appropriate clothing, and be sure it is immaculate. This is a business interview, and your appearance should indicate that you regard it as such. Besides, being well groomed and properly dressed will help boost your confidence.

Sooner or later, someone will call your name and escort you into the interview room. *This is it.* From here on you are on your own. It is too late for any more preparation. But remember, you asked for this opportunity to prove your fitness, and you are here because your request was granted.

What happens when you go in?

The usual sequence of events will be as follows: The clerk (who is often the board stenographer) will introduce you to the chairman of the oral board, who will introduce you to the other members of the board. Acknowledge the introductions before you sit down. Do not be surprised if you find a microphone facing you or a stenotypist sitting by. Oral interviews are usually recorded in the event of an appeal or other review.

Usually the chairman of the board will open the interview by reviewing the highlights of your education and work experience from your application – primarily for the benefit of the other members of the board, as well as to get the material into the record. Do not interrupt or comment unless there is an error or significant misinterpretation; if that is the case, do not hesitate. But do not quibble about insignificant matters. Also, he will usually ask you some question about your education, experience or your present job – partly to get you to start talking and to establish the interviewing "rapport." He may start the actual questioning, or turn it over to one of the other members. Frequently, each member undertakes the questioning on a particular area, one in which he is perhaps most competent, so you can expect each member to participate in the examination. Because time is limited, you may also expect some rather abrupt switches in the direction the questioning takes, so do not be upset by it. Normally, a board member will not pursue a single line of questioning unless he discovers a particular strength or weakness.

After each member has participated, the chairman will usually ask whether any member has any further questions, then will ask you if you have anything you wish to add. Unless you are expecting this question, it may floor you. Worse, it may start you off on an extended, extemporaneous speech. The board is not usually seeking more information. The question is principally to offer you a last opportunity to present further qualifications or to indicate that you have nothing to add. So, if you feel that a significant qualification or characteristic has been overlooked, it is proper to point it out in a sentence or so. Do not compliment the board on the thoroughness of their examination – they have been sketchy, and you know it. If you wish, merely say, "No thank you, I have nothing further to add." This is a point where you can "talk yourself out" of a good impression or fail to present an important bit of information. Remember, *you close the interview yourself.*

The chairman will then say, "That is all, Mr. ______, thank you." Do not be startled; the interview is over, and quicker than you think. Thank him, gather your belongings and take your leave. Save your sigh of relief for the other side of the door.

How to put your best foot forward

Throughout this entire process, you may feel that the board individually and collectively is trying to pierce your defenses, seek out your hidden weaknesses and embarrass and confuse you. Actually, this is not true. They are obliged to make an appraisal of your qualifications for the job you are seeking, and they want to see you in your best light. Remember, they must interview all candidates and a non-cooperative candidate may become a failure in spite of their best efforts to bring out his qualifications. Here are 15 suggestions that will help you:

1) Be natural – Keep your attitude confident, not cocky

If you are not confident that you can do the job, do not expect the board to be. Do not apologize for your weaknesses, try to bring out your strong points. The board is interested in a positive, not negative, presentation. Cockiness will antagonize any board member and make him wonder if you are covering up a weakness by a false show of strength.

2) Get comfortable, but don't lounge or sprawl

Sit erectly but not stiffly. A careless posture may lead the board to conclude that you are careless in other things, or at least that you are not impressed by the importance of the occasion. Either conclusion is natural, even if incorrect. Do not fuss with your clothing, a pencil or an ashtray. Your hands may occasionally be useful to emphasize a point; do not let them become a point of distraction.

3) Do not wisecrack or make small talk

This is a serious situation, and your attitude should show that you consider it as such. Further, the time of the board is limited – they do not want to waste it, and neither should you.

4) Do not exaggerate your experience or abilities

In the first place, from information in the application or other interviews and sources, the board may know more about you than you think. Secondly, you probably will not get away with it. An experienced board is rather adept at spotting such a situation, so do not take the chance.

5) If you know a board member, do not make a point of it, yet do not hide it

Certainly you are not fooling him, and probably not the other members of the board. Do not try to take advantage of your acquaintanceship – it will probably do you little good.

6) Do not dominate the interview

Let the board do that. They will give you the clues – do not assume that you have to do all the talking. Realize that the board has a number of questions to ask you, and do not try to take up all the interview time by showing off your extensive knowledge of the answer to the first one.

7) Be attentive

You only have 20 minutes or so, and you should keep your attention at its sharpest throughout. When a member is addressing a problem or question to you, give him your undivided attention. Address your reply principally to him, but do not exclude the other board members.

8) Do not interrupt

A board member may be stating a problem for you to analyze. He will ask you a question when the time comes. Let him state the problem, and wait for the question.

9) Make sure you understand the question

Do not try to answer until you are sure what the question is. If it is not clear, restate it in your own words or ask the board member to clarify it for you. However, do not haggle about minor elements.

10) Reply promptly but not hastily

A common entry on oral board rating sheets is "candidate responded readily," or "candidate hesitated in replies." Respond as promptly and quickly as you can, but do not jump to a hasty, ill-considered answer.

11) Do not be peremptory in your answers

A brief answer is proper – but do not fire your answer back. That is a losing game from your point of view. The board member can probably ask questions much faster than you can answer them.

12) Do not try to create the answer you think the board member wants

He is interested in what kind of mind you have and how it works – not in playing games. Furthermore, he can usually spot this practice and will actually grade you down on it.

13) Do not switch sides in your reply merely to agree with a board member

Frequently, a member will take a contrary position merely to draw you out and to see if you are willing and able to defend your point of view. Do not start a debate, yet do not surrender a good position. If a position is worth taking, it is worth defending.

14) Do not be afraid to admit an error in judgment if you are shown to be wrong

The board knows that you are forced to reply without any opportunity for careful consideration. Your answer may be demonstrably wrong. If so, admit it and get on with the interview.

15) Do not dwell at length on your present job

The opening question may relate to your present assignment. Answer the question but do not go into an extended discussion. You are being examined for a *new* job, not your present one. As a matter of fact, try to phrase ALL your answers in terms of the job for which you are being examined.

Basis of Rating

Probably you will forget most of these "do's" and "don'ts" when you walk into the oral interview room. Even remembering them all will not ensure you a passing grade. Perhaps you did not have the qualifications in the first place. But remembering them will help you to put your best foot forward, without treading on the toes of the board members.

Rumor and popular opinion to the contrary notwithstanding, an oral board wants you to make the best appearance possible. They know you are under pressure – but they also want to see how you respond to it as a guide to what your reaction would be under the pressures of the job you seek. They will be influenced by the degree of poise you display, the personal traits you show and the manner in which you respond.

ABOUT THIS BOOK

This book contains tests divided into Examination Sections. Go through each test, answering every question in the margin. At the end of each test look at the answer key and check your answers. On the ones you got wrong, look at the right answer choice and learn. Do not fill in the answers first. Do not memorize the questions and answers, but understand the answer and principles involved. On your test, the questions will likely be different from the samples. Questions are changed and new ones added. If you understand these past questions you should have success with any changes that arise. Tests may consist of several types of questions. We have additional books on each subject should more study be advisable or necessary for you. Finally, the more you study, the better prepared you will be. This book is intended to be the last thing you study before you walk into the examination room. Prior study of relevant texts is also recommended. NLC publishes some of these in our Fundamental Series. Knowledge and good sense are important factors in passing your exam. Good luck also helps. So now study this Passbook, absorb the material contained within and take that knowledge into the examination. Then do your best to pass that exam.

EXAMINATION SECTION

EXAMINATION SECTION

TEST 1

DIRECTIONS: Each question or incomplete statement is followed by several suggested answers or completions. Select the one that BEST answers the question or completes the statement. *PRINT THE LETTER OF THE CORRECT ANSWER IN THE SPACE AT THE RIGHT.*

1. The MAIN reason that a passenger should buy more than one fare at a time is to avoid 1.______
   A. errors in getting change each time
   B. waiting on a line each time
   C. train delays
   D. carrying too much change

2. It is reasonable to expect that a Station Agent would ordinarily be required to 2.______
   A. make minor repairs to the booth fan
   B. know how to use small tools
   C. hold disorderly passengers for the police
   D. know how to use the telephone

3. Of the following qualifications, the one MOST important for a Station Agent to have in the daily performance of his duties is 3.______
   A. knowledge of the rules governing his work
   B. ability to judge people
   C. a good knowledge of first aid practices
   D. ability to take charge in an emergency

4. A passenger asks for two fares and hands the railroad clerk ten dollars. 4.______
   If the fare is $2.75, the smallest number of bills the passenger can be given is
   A. 0 B. 2 C. 3 D. 4

5. An item that is owned by the City of New York is 5.______
   A. Fort Tilden B. Ellis Island
   C. Croton Reservoir D. Radio City

6. Each employee using supplies from one of the first aid kits throughout the subway is required to submit a report of the occurrence. 6.______
   The MOST likely reason for requiring this report is so that the
   A. employee may be given credit for his action
   B. used material will be sure to be replaced
   C. doctor can check if the proper first aid was given
   D. employee will use a first aid kit only when necessary

7. As an alert passenger, you have probably noticed that the third rail is 7.______
   A. one of the running rails
   B. located between the running rails
   C. suspended from the subway roof
   D. placed to one side of the running rails

8. The use of intoxicating liquor by employees while on duty is strictly prohibited by the rules of the transit authority MAINLY because the use of such liquor 8.______
   A. is expensive
   B. is immoral
   C. adversely affects their judgment
   D. causes a high rate of absenteeism

9. Safety on any job is BEST assured by 9.______
   A. working very slowly
   B. following every rule
   C. never working alone
   D. keeping alert

10. When official forms are to be filled out by employees, it is sometimes requested that certain information be printed rather than written MAINLY because printing 10.______
   A. is easier to do
   B. is legally required
   C. is more legible
   D. takes less space

11. Besides selling and adding value to fare cards and keeping a record of those sold, you would expect that the PRINCIPAL duty of a Station Agent is to 11.______
   A. keep records of turnstile readings
   B. receive lost property
   C. minimize vandalism near his booth
   D. call for an ambulance in an emergency

12. Of the following New York City parks, the one which is NOT located in the Borough of The Bronx is __________ Park. 12.______
   A. Pelham Bay
   B. Marine
   C. Crotona
   D. Van Cortland

13. The Verrazano Bridge connects Richmond AND 13.______
   A. Brooklyn
   B. Manhattan
   C. The Bronx
   D. Queens

14. As a safety feature, the edges of many subway station platforms are painted. The color of the paint used is GENERALLY 14.______
   A. green
   B. white
   C. red
   D. yellow

15. The BEST directions that can be given to a passenger are those which are 15.______
   A. direct and concise
   B. extremely detailed
   C. tactful
   D. lacking in details

Questions 16-25.

DIRECTIONS: Questions 16 through 25, inclusive, are based on the portion of a timetable shown below. Refer to this timetable in answering these questions.

TIMETABLE – *KK* LINE – WEEKDAYS

NORTHBOUND						SOUTHBOUND			
Train No.	Front St. Leave	Cane St. Leave	Amber St. Leave	Hall Square Arrive	Hall Square Leave	Amber St. Leave	Cane St. Leave	Front St. Arrive	Front St. Leave
76	7:25	7:35	7:45	8:00	8:05	8:20	8:30	8:40	8:45
77	7:40	7:50	8:00	8:15	8:20	8:35	8:45	8:55	9:00
78	7:55	8:05	8:15	8:30	8:35	8:50	9:00	9:10	9:15
79	8:05	8:15	8:25	8:40	8:45	9:00	9:10	9:20	9:25
80	8:15	8:25	8:35	8:50	8:55	9:10	9:20	9:30	9:35
81	8:25	8:35	8:45	9:00	9:05	9:20	9:30	9:40	9:45
82	8:35	8:45	8:55	9:10	9:15	9:30	9:40	9:50	9:55
76	8:45	8:55	9:05	9:20	9:25	9:40	9:50	10:00	10:05
83	P8:50	9:00	9:10	9:25	9:30	9:45	9:55	10:05	L
84	P8:55	9:05	9:15	9:30	9:35	9:50	10:00	10:10	10:15
77	9:00	9:10	9:20	9:35	9:40	9:55	10:05	10:15	L
85	P9:05	9:15	9:25	9:40	9:45	10:00	10:10	10:20	10:25
86	P9:10	9:20	9:30	9:45	9:50	10:05	10:15	10:25	L
78	9:15	9:25	9:35	9:50	9:55	10:10	10:20	10:30	10:35

NOTE: 1. P means that the train is put in passenger service at the location where P appears.
2. L means that the train is taken out of passenger service at the location where L appears.
3. Assume that the arrival times at Cane St. and Amber St. are the same as the leaving times.

16. If a passenger wishes to get to Hall Square station by 8:45 and is going to board the train at Cane St. station, he should plan to board the train which leaves this station at 16.______
A. 8:05 B. 8:15 C. 8:25 D. 8:30

17. For train No. 81, the total length of time, including the 5-minute layover at Hall Square, required for one round trip from Front St. to Hall Square and return is ______ minutes. 17.______
A. 70 B. 75 C. 80 D. 100

18. If a passenger arrives on the Amber St. station just before 9:00, he can expect to get to Front St. at 18.______
A. 8:05 B. 9:20 C. 9:25 D. 10:00

19. After 9:15, there is a train leaving Front St. every _______ minutes. 19._____
A. 5 B. 5 or 10 C. 10 D. 10 or 15

20. The TOTAL number of different train numbers listed in the portion of the timetable shown is 20._____
A. 14 B. 12 C. 11 D. 10

21. The length of time that trains are scheduled to remain at Hall Square is _______ minutes. 21._____
A. *always* 5 B. *always* 10 C. *always* 15 D. *either* 5 or 15

22. The TOTAL number of trains for which two complete round-trips are shown in the timetable is 22._____
A. 1 B. 2 C. 3 D. 4

23. The number of trains which are put in passenger service at Front St. that continue in service for more than one round-trip is 23._____
A. 4 B. 3 C. 2 D. 1

24. The TOTAL number of scheduled trains which pass Amber St. station in both directions from 8:30 to 9:00 is 24._____
A. 2 B. 4 C. 6 D. 8

25. From the timetable, you can infer that a number of storage tracks or a yard is located at or near 25._____
A. Front St. B. Hall Square C. Cane St. D. Amber St.

26. A passenger has fallen on the platform and apparently broken a leg. 26._____
Before calling for an ambulance, it would be BEST to
A. make him comfortable where he has fallen
B. apply a tourniquet
C. move him to a nearby bench and make him comfortable
D. ask him about the details of the accident

27. In 2015, it would be expected that the GREATEST number of passengers would use the subway on 27._____
A. Thursday, November 26 B. Monday, May 25
C. Monday, February 16 D. Tuesday, September 8

28. Station Agents were recently informed that a certain monthly school commutation ticket has a maroon colored date on a coral colored background. 28._____
The color maroon is BEST described as
A. olive green B. dark brown
C. pink D. dark brownish red

29. Referring to Question 28 above, the color coral is BEST described as 29._____
A. olive green B. dark brown
C. pink D. dark brownish red

30. Your supervisor supplies you with some paper forms on which you are to enter certain numerical data. 30.______
If you believe the forms supplied are not suitable for the purpose intended, it would be BEST for you to
A. substitute forms which you believe to be suitable
B. refuse to use the forms supplied
C. call this to your supervisor's attention immediately
D. consult another Station Agent on what to do

31. While a Station Agent is selling fare cards to a passenger, the passenger mutters something about poor subway service. 31.______
The Station Agent should take no action EXCEPT to
A. notify the transit police and let them handle the matter
B. try to obtain the passenger's name and address
C. ask the passenger to repeat his remarks
D. give the correct change, correct number of fare cards and ensure correct value is loaded on each card

32. When attempting to put out small fires on live electrical equipment, transit employees should use the chemical fire extinguisher rather than water MAINLY because 32.______
A. there is a water shortage in this area
B. water on a hot fire will generate poisonous fumes
C. water can conduct electricity and cause a shock hazard
D. water will cause corrosion of the electrical equipment

33. Station Agents are instructed to keep the booth door closed and locked. 33.______
The MAIN reason for this is to
A. protect them from angry passengers
B. protect them from cold drafts
C. prevent annoying distractions
D. make holdups more difficult

Questions 34-43.

DIRECTIONS: Questions 34 through 43, inclusive, are based on the description of an assumed accident given below. Read the description carefully before answering these questions.

<u>DESCRIPTION OF ACCIDENT</u>
(Taken from a newspaper dated October 21st)

Thirty-six persons were injured yesterday when a crowded Transit Authority bus and a white convertible collided in Brooklyn at about 2:20 P.M., at Frank and Boyd Streets.

Four persons, including Frieda Dorth, the 5-month-old daughter of Florence Dorth, are being treated for serious injuries at Blair Street Hospital. The other injured people were treated at nearby Brookside Hospital and sent home. The injured included persons in the bus and the car and a 10-year-old girl, Joyce Brand, who was standing on the sidewalk with her mother, Brenda, 27 years old, of 23 Charles Street, Brooklyn.

According to Patrolman Leo Gates, Badge 96287, of the 25th Precinct, the bus driven by James Bond, Badge 97528, was heading south on Frank Street when the automobile driven by Thomas Jones collided with the bus. Jones was only slightly hurt, but his passenger, Flora Smith, is in fair condition in Blair Street Hospital with a brain concussion. Thomas Jones was given a summons for going through a stop sign, using worn tires, and having an illegal registration.

34. The car that collided with the bus was a 34.______
A. sedan B. sports car
C. convertible D. station wagon

35. The number of people treated at Brookside Hospital was 35.______
A. 4 B. 5 C. 32 D. 36

36. This accident happened in the 36.______
A. early morning B. early afternoon
C. late morning D. late afternoon

37. The name of the mother of the seriously injured infant is 37.______
A. Florence B. Frieda C. Joyce D. Brenda

38. The name of the patrolman who reported on this accident is 38.______
A. James B. Frank C. Thomas D. Leo

39. It is clear that the 10-year-old girl 39.______
A. lives on Charles Street
B. was seriously injured
C. fell out of the passenger car
D. was a passenger on the bus

40. The number of violations for which the driver of the car was summoned is 40.______
A. 1 B. 2 C. 3 D. 4

41. The badge number of the Transit Authority bus driver is 41.______
A. 96287 B. 97528 C. 92687 D. 95728

42. The accident described took place on a 42.______
A. Tuesday B. Wednesday C. Thursday D. Friday

43. The patrolman who reported on this accident came from the _______ Precinct. 43.______
A. 23rd B. 24th C. 25th D. 27th

44. When the Station Agent is ready to leave the booth at the end of his tour of work, it would be MOST important for him to tell the person who is going to take charge of the booth about 44.______
A. a signal failure which caused a traffic delay
B. a turnstile at his location which is not working properly
C. a rumor that working hours may be reduced
D. the gang of men cleaning the walls of his station

45. When you are first appointed as a Station Agent, you are likely to be trained by working with an experienced Station Agent.
He will PROBABLY expect you to 45.______
A. do very little work
B. make plenty of mistakes
C. do all of the work
D. pay close attention to his instructions

46. According to BEST practice, Station Agent John Smith answering the telephone in the change booth at Dale Avenue station would say 46.______
A. "Dale Avenue, Station Agent Smith speaking"
B. "This is Smith – Who's calling?"
C. "Hello, this is Smith at Dale Avenue"
D. "Dale Avenue booth answering"

47. The legislation which was in the news and which should have been of particular interest to Station Agents is 47.______
A. medical care for the aged
B. one-man one-vote legislation
C. foreign aid
D. silver content of certain coins

48. An alert subway passenger would notice that some stations are brighter than others because of the use of 48.______
A. more lamps
B. fluorescent lamps
C. higher wattage lamps
D. flood lights

49. The passenger transportation facilities operated by the New York City Transit Authority are limited to subway 49.______
A. lines
B. and elevated lines
C. , elevated, and bus lines
D. , elevated, bus, and ferry lines

50. After giving you an order over the phone, your supervisor is likely to ask you to repeat it back to him to make sure that you 50.______
A. will carry out the order as given
B. are the Station Agent on duty
C. heard the order correctly
D. have written the order down

8.(#1)

KEY (CORRECT ANSWERS)

1. A	16. B	31. D	46. A
2. D	17. B	32. C	47. D
3. A	18. B	33. D	48. B
4. B	19. C	34. C	49. C
5. C	20. C	35. C	50. C
6. B	21. A	36. B	
7. D	22. C	37. A	
8. C	23. C	38. D	
9. D	24. C	39. A	
10. C	25. A	40. C	
11. A	26. A	41. B	
12. B	27. D	42. B	
13. A	28. D	43. C	
14. D	29. C	44. B	
15. A	30. C	45. D	

TEST 2

DIRECTIONS: Each question or incomplete statement is followed by several suggested answers or completions. Select the one that BEST answers the question or completes the statement. *PRINT THE LETTER OF THE CORRECT ANSWER IN THE SPACE AT THE RIGHT.*

Questions 1-10.

DIRECTIONS: Questions 1 through 10 refer to the arithmetic examples shown in the boxes below. Be sure to refer to the proper box when answering each question.

3849 728 3164 773 32	18.70 268.38 17.64 9.40	66788 8639	154 x 48	32.56 x 8.6
BOX 1	BOX 2	BOX 3	BOX 4	BOX 5
$34\overline{)2890}$	32.49 – 8.7	\$582.17 -38.58	\$6.72 ÷ \$0.24	3/8 X 264
BOX 6	BOX 7	BOX 8	BOX 9	BOX 10

1. The sum of the five numbers in Box 1 is 1.______
   A. 7465 B. 7566 C. 8465 D. 8546

2. The sum of the four numbers in Box 2 is 2.______
   A. 341.21 B. 341.12 C. 314.21 D. 314.12

3. The difference between the two numbers in Box 3 is 3.______
   A. 75427 B. 74527 C. 58149 D. 57149

4. The product of the two numbers in Box 4 is 4.______
   A. 1232 B. 6160 C. 7392 D. 8392

5. The product of the two numbers in Box 5 is 5.______
   A. 28.016 B. 280.016 C. 280.16 D. 2800.16

6. The result of the division indicated in Box 6 is 6.______
   A. 85 B. 850 C. 8.5 D. 185

7. The difference between the two numbers in Box 7 is 7.______
   A. 23.79 B. 21.53 C. 19.97 D. 18.79

8. The difference between the two numbers in Box 8 is 8.______
A. $620.75 B. $602.59 C. $554.75 D. $543.59

9. The result of the division indicated in Box 9 is 9.______
A. .0357 B. 28.0 C. 280 D. 35.7

10. The product of the two numbers in Box 10 is 10.______
A. 9.90 B. 89.0 C. 99.0 D. 199.

Questions 11-20.

DIRECTIONS: Questions 11 through 20 in Column I are important highways and places of interest in New York City, each of which is located in one of the boroughs listed in Column II. Indicate the correspondingly numbered row in the space at the right the letter preceding your selected borough.

COLUMN I	COLUMN II	
11. Grand Concourse	A. Manhattan	11.______
12. Grand Army Plaza	B. The Bronx	12.______
13. Grand Central Parkway	C. Brooklyn	13.______
14. Citi Field	D. Queens	14.______
15. Kennedy Airport		15.______
16. Hayden Planetarium		16.______
17. Fort Hamilton		17.______
18. Manhattan College		18.______
19. Erie Basin		19.______
20. Metropolitan Museum of Art		20.______

21. It is generally true that MOST accidents to employees result from 21.______
A. too heavy work schedules
B. carelessness
C. poor light
D. insufficient knowledge about the work

22. You will probably be appreciated MOST by your superior if you 22.______
A. frequently ask him questions about your job
B. often make suggestions about improving the working condition
C. tell him every time any co-worker has violated a rule
D. do your work accurately and on time

23. In most cases, the logical and proper source from which you should first seek explanation of a written order which you do NOT understand would be the 23.______
A. Transit Authority legal department
B. general superintendent
C. book of rules
D. person who is your immediate superior

24. An order addressed to *All Concerned* states that a certain order issued earlier has been revoked. 24.______
This means MOST NEARLY that the earlier order has been
A. annulled or withdrawn
B. updated and put into effect immediately
C. sent to the proper authority for further study
D. reissued to emphasize its importance to all concerned

25. A transit system rule states that a Station Agent must give notice of his intention to be absent from work at least one hour before he is scheduled to report for duty. 25.______
The MOST logical reason for having this rule is so that
A. the Station Agent's excuse can be checked
B. a substitute can be provided
C. the payroll department can be notified promptly
D. a Station Agent will realize that this job is important

26. When summoning an ambulance for an injured person, it is MOST important to give the 26.______
A. location of the injured person
B. nature of the injuries
C. cause of the accident
D. name of the injured person

27. Signs in the subway forbid passengers to 27.______
A. carry any packages
B. run upstairs
C. talk to the conductor
D. cross the tracks

28. The weekly pay of a railroad clerk for 8 hours a day, 5 days a week, at $15.09 an hour is 28.______
A. $591.60
B. $603.60
C. $636.00
D. $639.60

29. A passenger using the A Division lines on his way to Staten Island should get off at 29.______
A. Cortlandt St.
B. Fulton St.
C. South Ferry
D. Canal St.

Questions 30-36.

DIRECTIONS: Questions 30 through 36, inclusive, refer to the Tabulation of Turnstile Readings shown below, and to the note given beneath the tabulation. Refer to this tabulation and the note in answering these questions.

TABULATION OF TURNSTILE READINGS

Turnstile Number	TURNSTILE READINGS AT					
	5:30 A.M.	6:00 A.M.	7:00 A.M.	8:00 A.M.	9:00 A.M.	9:30 A.M.
1	79078	79090	79225	79590	79860	79914
2	24915	24930	25010	25441	25996	26055
3	39509	39530	39736	40533	41448	41515
4	58270	58291	58396	58958	59729	59807
5	43371	43378	43516	43888	44151	44217

Note: 1. The turnstiles register the number of passengers.

30. The number of passengers using turnstile No. 1 from 8:00 A.M. to 9:00 A.M. was 30.______
A. 150 B. 270 C. 350 D. 370

31. The TOTAL number of passengers using turnstile No. 5 from opening to closing was 31.______
A. 846 B. 1140 C. 1537 D. 2005

32. The number of passengers using turnstile No. 2 in the last half hour was 32.______
A. 59 B. 67 C. 270 D. 314

33. The MOST used turnstile from opening to closing was No. 33.______
A. 2 B. 3 C. 4 D. 5

34. The turnstile used by the LEAST passengers from 6:00 A.M. to 7:00 A.M. was No. 34.______
A. 4 B. 3 C. 2 D. 1

35. From 5:30 A.M. to 7:00 A.M., the Station Agent sold exactly 525 fares. The cash taken in for the 525 fares was (assuming $2 fare) 35.______
A. $1575.00 B. $1050.00 C. $315.00 D. $115.00

36. The peak load on turnstile No. 5 is between 36.______
A. 5:30 A.M. and 6:00 A.M. B. 6:00 A.M. and 7:00 A.M.
C. 7:00 A.M. and 8:00 A.M. D. 8:00 A.M. and 9:00 A.M.

37. In New York, daylight saving time ends near the end of 37.______
A. March B. April C. September D. October

38. There is no subway station at 42nd St. AND 38.______
A. Lexington Ave. B. 3rd Ave.
C. 6th Ave. D. 8th Ave.

Questions 39-46.

DIRECTIONS: Questions 39 through 46 are based on the paragraphs about accident statistics given below. Read these statistics carefully before answering these questions.

ACCIDENT STATISTICS

Accidents are among our nation's leading killers, maulers, and money wasters. In the United States during 2013, according to the National Safety Council figures, there wera 100,000 fatal accidents of all kinds, and ten million various types of disabling injuries. Some 40,000 deaths involved motor vehicles. The home accounted for 29,000 fatalities, and public places 17,000. There were 14,000 deaths and two million disabling injuries in industry.

In 2003, the total cost of accidents in the United States was at least 16 billion dollars. For industry alone, the cost of accidents was 5 billion dollars, equal to $70 per worker. The total time lost was about 230 million man-days of work.

39. The statistics quoted above are for 39.______
A. the home *only*
B. the entire United States
C. New York State
D. New York City

40. The statistics quoted above are for the year 40.______
A. 2010
B. 2011
C. 2012
D. 2013

41. Of the 100,000 fatal accidents of all kinds, those NOT involved with motor vehicles totaled 41.______
A. 17,000
B. 29,000
C. 40,000
D. 60,000

42. The number of disabling injuries of all kinds which were listed for industry was _______ million. 42.______
A. 10
B. 8
C. 4
D. 2

43. Accidents cost our nation AT LEAST _______ dollars. 43.______
A. 16 billion
B. 5 billion
C. 10 million
D. 2 million

44. The number of deaths due to accidents in the home was close to 44.______
A. 15,000
B. 20,000
C. 30,000
D. 40,000

45. The number of deaths per day from accidents of all kinds averaged about 45.______
A. 275
B. 300
C. 325
D. 350

46. During the year for which these statistics are given, the cost of industrial accidents per worker was 46.______
A. $230
B. $70
C. $17
D. $5

47. The 42nd Street Shuttle train runs to 47.______
A. Union Square
B. Grand Central
C. Penn Station
D. Columbus Circle

48. The carrying of large packages into the subway is forbidden MAINLY to prevent 48.______
A. overloading the cars
B. trucking industry objections
C. interference with passenger movement
D. platform littering

49. For many years, efforts have been made by the city to have employers stagger the working hours of their employees in order to 49.______
A. reduce rush hour congestion
B. increase subway revenue
C. give employees more time for recreation
D. enable the present equipment to carry more passengers

50. Safety rules are useful because they 50.______
A. place the responsibility for an accident on an employee
B. make it necessary to concentrate
C. prevent carelessness
D. are a guide to avoid common dangers

KEY (CORRECT ANSWERS)

1. D	16. A	31. A	46. B
2. D	17. C	32. A	47. B
3. C	18. B	33. B	48. C
4. C	19. C	34. C	49. A
5. B	20. A	35. B	50. D
6. A	21. B	36. C	
7. A	22. D	37. D	
8. D	23. D	38. B	
9. B	24. A	39. B	
10. C	25. B	40. D	
11. B	26. A	41. D	
12. C	27. D	42. D	
13. D	28. B	43. A	
14. D	29. C	44. C	
15. D	30. B	45. A	

TEST 3

DIRECTIONS: Each question or incomplete statement is followed by several suggested answers or completions. Select the one that BEST answers the question or completes the statement. *PRINT THE LETTER OF THE CORRECT ANSWER IN THE SPACE AT THE RIGHT.*

1. Subway employees are required to be courteous to the public MAINLY because it 1.______
   A. makes the employees more efficient
   B. is the best way to get people to use the subways
   C. makes the job more pleasant
   D. is a logical part of the service rendered for the fare

2. Station Agents should 2.______
   A. personally try and sell as many tokens as possible
   B. tidy up the area near their booth when things are slow
   C. be able to advise passengers how to get to desired places
   D. make a daily comparison between passengers exiting at his station

3. If a Station Agent notices a person in the station acting in a definitely suspicious manner, the Station Agent should 3.______
   A. go to the person and question him
   B. ignore the matter and wait for developments
   C. request a passenger to investigate
   D. call the transit police and report the matter

Questions 4-10.

DIRECTIONS: Questions 4 through 10 refer to the Tabulation of Turnstile Readings shown below and to the notes given beneath the tabulation. Refer to this tabulation and the notes in answering these questions.

TABULATION OF TURNSTILE READINGS

Turnstile Number	TURNSTILE READINGS AT					
	5:30 A.M.	6:00 A.M.	7:00 A.M.	8:00 A.M.	9:00 A.M.	10:00 A.M.
1	38921	38931	39064	39435	39704	39843
2	67463	67486	67592	68148	68917	69058
3	65387	65408	65611	66414	67324	67461
4	22538	22542	22631	23061	23613	23720

NOTE: 1. Turnstiles are operated by tokens costing $2.00 each.
2. The subway entrance at which these turnstiles are located is open, with a Station Agent on duty from 5:30 A.M. to 10:00 A.M.

4. The number of passengers using turnstile No. 3 from 7:00 A.M. to 8:00 A.M. was 4.______
   A. 203 B. 803 C. 910 D. 1197

5. The turnstile used by the MOST passengers from 8:00 A.M. to 9:00 A.M. was No. 5.______
A. 1 B. 2 C. 3 D. 4

6. The number of passengers using turnstile No. 4 in the FIRST half hour was 6.______
A. 4 B. 10 C. 21 D. 23

7. The TOTAL number of passengers using turnstile No. 2 from opening to closing was 7.______
A. 922 B. 1182 C. 1595 D. 2074

8. The MOST used turnstile from opening to closing was No. 8.______
A. 1 B. 2 C. 3 D. 4

9. From 8:00 A.M. to 9:00 A.M., the Station Agent sold exactly 1000 fares, while the turnstile readings for the four turnstiles show that a total of 2500 passengers passed through them in the same period. 9.______
The number of passengers who purchased fares was MOST probably
A. less than 1000 B. exactly 1000
C. between 1000 and 1500 D. exactly 2500

10. The cash taken in for the 1000 fares of Question 9 was 10.______
A. $900.00 B. $1000.00 C. $2000.00 $3000.00

11. Radio City is located nearest to 11.______
A. Columbus Circle B. Queens Plaza
C. Hudson Terminal D. Union Square

12. A Station Agent would be MOST directly involved in case of a passenger who 12.______
A. collapsed at a turnstile
B. was struck by a car door
C. was overcome by smoke in an under-river tunnel
D. fell on the street at the entrance to the subway

Questions 13-22.

DIRECTIONS: Questions 13 through 22, inclusive, are based on the portion of a timetable shown below. Refer to this timetable in answering these questions.

TIMETABLE – *HH* LINE – WEEKDAYS

NORTHBOUND						SOUTHBOUND			
Train No.	Hall St. Leave	Ann St. Leave	Best St. Leave	Knob Avenue Arrive	Knob Avenue Leave	Best St. Leave	Ann St. Leave	Hall St. Arrive	Hall St. Leave
88	7:35	7:50	8:05	8:15	8:20	8:30	8:45	9:00	9:05
89	7:50	8:05	8:20	8:30	8:35	8:45	9:00	9:15	9:20
90	8:05	8:20	8:35	8:45	8:50	9:00	9:15	9:30	9:35
91	8:20	8:35	8:50	9:00	9:05	9:15	9:30	9:45	9:50
92	8:30	8:45	9:00	9:10	9:15	9:25	9:40	9:55	10:00
93	8:40	8:55	9:10	9:20	9:25	9:35	9:50	10:05	10:10
94	8:50	9:05	9:20	9:30	9:35	9:45	10:00	10:15	10:20
95	9:00	9:15	9:30	9:40	9:45	9:55	10:10	10:25	10:30
88	9:05	9:20	9:35	9:45	9:50	10:00	10:15	10:30	LU*
96	9:10	9:25	9:40	9:50	9:55	10:05	10:20	10:35	10:40
97	9:15	9:30	9:45	9:55	10:00	10:10	10:25	10:40	LU*
89	9:20	9:35	9:50	10:00	10:05	10:15	10:30	10:45	10:50

NOTE: LU* means that the train is taken out of passenger service at the location where LU appears.
Assume that the arrival times at Ann St. and Best St. are the same as the leaving times.

13. The TOTAL number of different train numbers listed in the portion of the timetable shown is — 13.______
A. 9 B. 10 C. 11 D. 12

14. For train No. 95, the average of the running times from Hall St. to Ann St., from Ann St. to Best St., and from Best St. to Knob Ave., is about _______ minutes. — 14.______
A. 12 B. 13 C. 14 D. 15

15. A passenger leaving Hall St. on the 7:50 train is going to Knob Ave. to take care of some business. — 15.______
If his business takes a total of one hour, he can be back at Hall St. by about
A. 8:50 B. 9:20 C. 10:15 D. 10:40

16. A passenger reaching Ann St. at 9:17 to leave on a northbound train would expect to arrive at Knob Ave. at — 16.______
A. 9:35 B. 9:45 C. 9:50 D. 10:15

17. The TOTAL number of trains for which two complete round-trips are shown in the timetable is — 17.______
A. 4 B. 3 C. 2 D. 1

18. A person reaching Best St. at 9:03 to board a southbound train would have to wait until 18.______
A. 9:05 B. 9:10 C. 9:15 D. 9:20

19. The length of time required for any train to make the northbound run from Hall St. to Knob Ave. is _______ minutes. 19.______
A. 40 B. 45 C. 50 D. 85

20. The length of time that trains are scheduled to remain at Hall St. is _______ minutes. 20.______
A. *always* 5 B. *always* 10
C. *always* 15 D. *either* 5 or 10

21. From the entries in the timetable, you can infer that the location near which there is MOST likely to be a subway yard to store trains is 21.______
A. Ann St. B. Best St. C. Knob Ave. D. Hall St.

22. For train No. 91, the TOTAL length of time, including the 5-minute layover at Knob Ave., required for one round-trip from Hall St. to Knob Ave. and return is _______ minutes. 22.______
A. 80 B. 85 C. 90 D. 120

Questions 23-32.

DIRECTIONS: Questions 23 through 32 in Column I are the names of well-known places in the City, each of which is situated in one of the four boroughs listed in Column II. For each name in Column I, select the borough in which it is situated from Column II.

COLUMN I	COLUMN II	
23. Bowling Green	A. The Bronx	23.______
24. Aqueduct Race Track	B. Brooklyn	24.______
25. Flushing Meadow Park	C. Manhattan	25.______
26. Manhattan Beach	D. Queens	26.______
27. Washington Square		27.______
28. Pelham Bay Park		28.______
29. City Hall		29.______
30. Woodlawn Cemetery		30.______
31. Canarsie Beach Park		31.______
32. La Guardia Airport		32.______

33. There is a rule that unauthorized employees are prohibited from entering on the subway tracks. 33.______
The BASIC reason for this rule is that the practice
A. is dangerous
B. is objectionable
C. is unlawful
D. interferes with train service

34. In 2015, it would be expected that the GREATEST number of passengers would use the subway on 34.______
A. Thursday, November 26
B. Friday, December 25
C. Monday, October 12
D. Tuesday, May 26

35. A passenger asks for two tokens and hands the Station Agent ten dollars. 35.______
The SMALLEST number of bills the passenger can be given in change is
A. 2
B. 3
C. 4
D. 5

36. The fact that Station Agents must be acceptable for bonding would MOST probably disqualify a person 36.______
A. who had numerous charge accounts
B. who is nearsighted
C. who had only handled small amounts of money
D. with a record of money irregularities

37. The BEST way for the average regular subway passenger to avoid the annoyance of waiting in line to buy fares is to buy them on a _______ the subway. 37.______
A. weekly basis when entering
B. daily basis when leaving
C. weekly basis when leaving
D. daily basis when entering

38. There is a free subway transfer point at Columbus Circle. This transfer is between _______ lines. 38.______
A. Broadway and 6th Ave.
B. Broadway and Lexington Ave.
C. Broadway-7th Ave. and 8th Ave.
D. Broadway, 63rd St. and Lexington Ave.

39. By logical reasoning, it can be concluded that the PRINCIPAL duty of a Station Agent who is assigned to an exit gate is to 39.______
A. prevent cheating
B. give directions
C. sell fares
D. eliminate crowding

40. To change from Daylight Saving Time to Standard Time, the hands of the clock are moved 40.______
A. ahead in autumn
B. back in autumn
C. back in spring
D. ahead in spring

41. A location which is city-owned is 41.______
A. Statue of Liberty
B. New York Naval Shipyard
C. Central Park
D. Radio City

42. The official rules prohibit a baby carriage containing a baby from being admitted into the subway. 42.______
This is MAINLY because the
A. baby may become sick
B. carriage would be difficult to get through the controls
C. carriage is likely to interfere with passengers
D. baby may be crushed

43. On checking a pile of tickets arranged in numerical order, you find that the next ticket after number 17,474 is number 17,747. 43.______
The number of tickets missing is
A. 171 B. 272 C. 373 D. 474

44. For many years, efforts have continuously been made by the city and by various civic organizations to have employers stagger the working hours of their employees in order to 44.______
A. reduce rush hour congestion
B. increase subway revenue
C. give employees more time for recreation
D. have the trains carry more people

Questions 45-50.

DIRECTIONS: Questions 45 through 50 are based on the Bulletin Order given below. Refer to this bulletin order when answering these questions.

BULLETIN ORDER NO. 67

SUBJECT: Procedure for Handling Fire Occurrences 6-17---

In order that the Fire Department may be notified of all fires, even those that have been extinguished by our own employees, any employee having knowledge of a fire must notify the Station Department Office immediately on telephone extensions: D-4177, D-4181, D-4185, or D-4189.

Specific information regarding the fire should include the location of the fire, the approximate distance north or south of the nearest station, and the track designation, line, and division.

In addition, the report should contain information as to the status of the fire and whether our forces have extinguished it or if Fire Department equipment is required.

When all information has been obtained, the Station Supervisor in Charge in the Station Department Office will notify the Desk Trainmaster of the Division involved.

Richard Roe,
Superintendent

45. An employee having knowledge of a fire should FIRST notify the 45.______
A. Station Department Office B. Fire Department
C. Desk Trainmaster D. Station Supervisor

46. If Bulletin Order No. 1 was issued on January 2, bulletins are being issued at the monthly average of 46.______
A. 8 B. 10 C. 12 D. 14

47. It is clear from the Bulletin that 47.______
A. employees are expected to be expert fire fighters
B. many fires occur on the transit system
C. train service is usually suspended whenever a fire occurs
D. some fires are extinguished without the help of the Fire Department

48. From the information furnished in this Bulletin, it can be assumed that the 48.______
A. Station Department Office handles a considerable number of telephone calls
B. Superintendent investigates the handling of all subway fires
C. Fire Department is notified only in case of large fires
D. employee first having knowledge of the fire must call all four extensions

49. The probable reason for notifying the Fire Department even when the fire has been extinguished by a subway employee is because the Fire Department is 49.______
A. a city agency
B. still responsible to check the fire
C. concerned with fire prevention
D. required to clean up after the fire

50. Information about the fire NOT specifically required is 50.______
A. track B. time of day
C. station D. division

KEY (CORRECT ANSWERS)

1. D	16. B	31. B	46. C
2. C	17. C	32. D	47. D
3. D	18. C	33. A	48. A
4. B	19. A	34. D	49. C
5. C	20. A	35. A	50. B
6. A	21. D	36. D	
7. C	22. B	37. C	
8. C	23. C	38. C	
9. A	24. D	39. A	
10. C	25. D	40. B	
11. A	26. B	41. C	
12. A	27. C	42. C	
13. B	28. A	43. B	
14. B	29. C	44. A	
15. C	30. A	45. A	

TEST 4

DIRECTIONS: Each question or incomplete statement is followed by several suggested answers or completions. Select the one that BEST answers the question or completes the statement. *PRINT THE LETTER OF THE CORRECT ANSWER IN THE SPACE AT THE RIGHT.*

Questions 1-10.

DIRECTIONS: Questions 1 through 10 refer to the arithmetic examples shown in the boxes below. Be sure to refer to the proper box when answering each question.

23.3 – 5.72 BOX 1	$491.26 -127.47 BOX 2	$7.95 ÷ $0.15 BOX 3	4758 1639 2075 864 23 BOX 4	27.6 179.47 8.73 46.5 BOX 5
243 x 57 BOX 6	57697 - 9748 BOX 7	23.65 x 9.7 BOX 8	3/4 x 260 BOX 9	25 $\sqrt{1975}$ BOX 10

1. The difference between the two numbers in Box 1 is 1.______
   A. 17.42 B. 17.58 C. 23.35 D. 29.02

2. The difference between the two numbers in Box 2 is 2.______
   A. $274.73 B. $363.79 C. $374.89 D. $618.73

3. The result of the division indicated in Box 3 is 3.______
   A. $0.53 B. $5.30 C. 5.3 D. 53

4. The sum of the five numbers in Box 4 is 4.______
   A. 8355 B. 9359 C. 9534 D. 10359

5. The sum of the four numbers in Box 5 is 5.______
   A. 262.30 B. 272.03 C. 372.23 D. 372.30

6. The product of the two numbers in Box 6 is 6.______
   A. 138.51 B. 1385.1 C. 13851 D. 138510

7. The difference between the two numbers in Box 7 is 7.______
   A. 67445 B. 48949 C. 47949 D. 40945

8. The product of the two numbers in Box 8 is 8.______
   A. 22.9405 B. 229.405 C. 2294.05 D. 229405

9. The product of the two numbers in Box 9 is 9.______
A. 65 B. 120 C. 195 D. 240

10. The result of the division indicated in Box 10 is 10.______
A. 790 B. 379 C. 179 D. 79

11. The subway station which is NEAREST to Madison Square Garden is _______ Line. 11.______
A. 50th St. on the 8th Ave. Local
B. 59th St. on the Broadway-7th Ave.
C. 49th St. on the Brighton Line
D. 50th St. on the 6th Ave. Express

12. As compared with salt, the use of sand on icy station stairways is 12.______
A. more effective B. more expensive
C. less corrosive D. less work

13. The Transit Authority has MOST recently been conducting a vigorous campaign to 13.______
A. keep the subways clean
B. promote courtesy
C. have passengers buy tokens in large quantities
D. increase the number of riders

14. A Station Agent should be MOST concerned if a passenger tells him that 14.______
A. trains are running behind schedule
B. he lost a nickel in a vending machine
C. there is no soap in the men's room
D. a small child is wandering around the platform unattended

15. There is a free subway transfer point at Times Square. This transfer is between the 15.______
A. Broadway and 8th Ave. lines
B. Broadway Line and 42nd St. Shuttle
C. 8th Ave. and Flushing Line
D. Broadway-7th Ave., Flushing, Broadway, 8th Ave. lines and 42nd St. Shuttle

16. Station Agents should realize that transit employees become acquainted with new regulations MAINLY through 16.______
A. notices posted on bulletin boards
B. verbal orders from their superiors
C. re-issues of the book of rules
D. talking to co-workers

17. In making a report concerning an accident which took place on a stairway from the mezzanine to the train platform at a subway station, the LEAST important item to include is the 17.______
A. time of day B. date
C. number of steps D. weather

18. It had been suggested that the $2.75 fares used for rides on the subway should be sold in packages. 18.______
Under such a plan, the LARGEST saving to the riders would be if the fares were sold for
A. 2 for $5.25
B. 3 for $8.00
C. 5 for $13.50
D. 7 for $19.00

19. Station Agents are prohibited from taking razor blades into a change booth. 19.______
The MOST likely reason is that the razor blades
A. are fragile and easily broken
B. are personal property
C. are not required by the clerks in the discharge of their duties
D. may cause an accident

20. The subway line which uses a bridge over the East River for some of its service is the _______ line. 20.______
A. IND Washington Heights
B. IRT Lexington Ave.
C. BMT Brighton
D. IND Rockaway

Questions 21-27.

DIRECTIONS: Questions 21 through 27 are based on the article given below. Refer to this article when answering these questions.

ARTICLE NO. 123

CHANGE BOOTH CLASSIFICATION AND DESIGNATION

1. 24-Hour Booth. Any booth manned continuously

2. Part-time Booth. Any booth ordinarily manned for less than 24 hours in one day.

3. Station Head Booth. One 24-hour booth in each station at which the railroad clerk is in general charge of the station and, in some cases, from which a part-time booth funds and block tickets are drawn.

4. Area Control Booth. A 24-hour booth at which night lunch reliefs report "in" and "out" and which is a lost property depository point where mail is delivered to and from and, in some cases, from which part-time booth funds and block tickets are drawn.

5. Transfer Booth. A 24-hour booth or part-time booth allocated for the exclusive handling of transfers.

21. All subway stations have a booth classified as number 21.______
A. 2 B. 3 C. 4 D. 5

22. The block tickets referred to would MOST likely be used for 22.______
A. substitution of tokens when the supply is exhausted
B. temporary interruption in train service
C. refunding purposes in case of a stuck turnstile
D. issuance to passengers who complain about train service

23. It is evident that there would NOT be any money kept in a booth classified as number 23.______
A. 2 B. 3 C. 4 D. 5

24. From the information furnished in this article, it can CORRECTLY be said that 24.______
A. transfer booths are always open 24 hours a day
B. station head booths are more important than area control booths
C. money is not left in an unattended booth
D. mail is delivered to the area control booth by the night lunch relief man

25. A Station Agent in a number 5 booth is informed by a passenger that he left a package on the subway station bench the previous night. 25.______
The passenger should be directed to the NEAREST booth classified as number
A. 1 B. 2 C. 3 D. 4

26. A logical conclusion is that 26.______
A. booths classified as number 2 are used in non-rush hours
B. there are more change booths than there are stations
C. the size of a booth determines its classification
D. there are transfers handled at all stations

27. The Station Agent who would have the MOST authority at a station would be at a booth classified as number 27.______
A. 1 B. 3 C. 4 D. 5

28. Official photographers for the various New York newspapers do not require special permission to take pictures on the stations of the city transit system. 28.______
A LIKELY reason for this procedure is that
A. the station is not a restricted area
B. all publicity is good
C. of the freedom of the press
D. it provides free advertising

29. There is a free transfer point between all three subway divisions at 29.______
A. Coney Island B. Herald Square
C. Broadway-Nassau St. D. Broadway-168th St.

30. It is CORRECT to say that the 30.______
A. Lincoln Tunnel is under the East River
B. George Washington Bridge connects Manhattan and New Jersey
C. Williamsburgh Bridge is near Yankee Stadium
D. Queens-Midtown Tunnel is under the Harlem River

31. A recent Transit Authority bulletin states that *A smile has more than its face value. It takes 65 muscles to frown and only 13 to smile.* 31.______
From the form of this statement, it can logically be concluded that the MAIN purpose is to
A. be humorous
B. have employees smile at all times
C. provide medical information
D. make an effective impact on the employees

32. It is customary during each year for hourly turnstile meter readings to be taken on a typical day of the week for a 3 or 4 week period. 32.______
Such readings would be MOST useful to
A. reveal the passenger pattern for the day
B. keep the Station Agents busy
C. act as a check on the performance of the Station Agents
D. show if additional change booths are needed

33. The GREATEST number of subway lines operate through the borough of 33.______
A. Bronx B. Brooklyn C. Manhattan D. Queens

34. The subway line which ONLY operates east and west is the 34.______
A. IND Crosstown B. BMT Franklin Ave. Shuttle
C. IRT Flushing D. IRT 42nd St. Shuttle

35. A passenger tendered a Station Agent twenty dollars and asked for six tokens. In the change returned by the clerk, the passenger received one five-dollar bill and four one-dollar bills. 35.______
In this case, the Station Agent gave the passenger
A. one dollar too little B. the correct change
C. one dollar too much D. two dollars too much

36. On the official printed forms prepared by the Station Agents, their names must be both printed and signed. 36.______
The reason for the signature is for the purpose of
A. authenticity B. simplicity
C. neatness D. correctness

37. The article turned in to a Station Agent which would MOST likely require special handling is a(n) 37.______
A. empty wallet B. umbrella
C. pair of shoes D. frozen turkey

38. There is a subway station at Penn. Station on the _______ Line. 38.______
A. BMT Sea Beach B. IRT Broadway
C. IND 6th Ave. D. IRT Flushing

39. At a subway station located in the financial district, the turnstile readings would MOST likely show the GREATEST number of passengers entering the station between the hours of _______ and _______. 39.______
A. 8:00 A.M.; 10:00 A.M. B. 10:00 A.M.; 12 Noon
C. 4:00 P.M.; 6:00 P.M. D. 6:00 P.M.; 8:00 P.M.

40. The Port of New York Authority constructed a bus terminal at 40.______
A. 179th St. and Broadway B. Grand Central Station
C. Erie Basin D. 34th St. and 7th Ave.

41. A recent newspaper article stated that millions of riders had not returned to the city transit system. 41.______
The reason given for the decrease in the number of riders was
A. dirtier subways
B. cost of ridership
C. subway crime
D. defaced cars and buses

42. The LATEST subway maps which are displayed at stations do NOT show which 42.______
A. lines give part-time service only
B. boroughs the subway lines are located
C. stations call for an extra fare
D. stations are located on elevated structures

43. Station Agents have either day or night assignments, selecting their tour of duty by a seniority pick. 43.______
The MOST probable reason for using this method is to
A. reward length of service
B. give every employee the assignment he desires
C. encourage new employees
D. avoid difficulty in filling assignments

44. If a passenger asks you how to reach a certain destination with which you are not acquainted, your BEST procedure would be to 44.______
A. tell him you do not know
B. look it up if possible
C. tell him to ask some passenger
D. call the police precinct

45. Members of the city police and fire departments, when in uniform or upon presentation of their badges, will be carried free on the transit system. 45.______
The reason for this is that
A. they are easy to identify
B. they are city employees
C. their rate of pay is low
D. they travel a considerable amount on official business

46. A subway line which has a station at Yankee Stadium is the _______ Line. 46.______
A. IND *BB*
B. IRT Pelham Bay
C. IND *A*
D. IRT Jerome Ave.

47. A Station Agent must pass a color vision test before appointment. 47.______
One reason is that
A. it is a measure of his general health
B. various colored passes are used for free transportation on the subway system
C. he may be offered counterfeit money in payment for tokens
D. bulletin orders are sometimes printed on colored paper.

48. If a passenger at the change booth complains about the service, the Station Agent should 48.______
A. refrain from arguing
B. call his immediate supervisor
C. ask him for his name and address
D. argue him out of his mood

49. The recommended first-aid procedure for a person who has fainted is to lay him down with his head lower than his body. 49.______
Such a position is used because it
A. quickly relieves exhaustion
B. is the most comfortable position
C. speeds the return of blood to his head
D. retards rapid breathing

50. If an ambulance is required for an injured passenger, all subway employees, including Station Agents, are instructed to call the transit police department and have them call the ambulance. 50.______
An IMPORTANT reason for such a procedure is to
A. enable the clerk to concentrate on his regular duties
B. provide faster service
C. fix responsibility
D. avoid possible duplication of calls

KEY (CORRECT ANSWERS)

1. B	16. A	31. D	46. D
2. B	17. C	32. A	47. B
3. D	18. A	33. C	48. A
4. B	19. D	34. D	49. C
5. A	20. C	35. C	50. D
6. C	21. B	36. A	
7. C	22. B	37. D	
8. B	23. D	38. B	
9. C	24. C	39. C	
10. D	25. D	40. A	
11. A	26. B	41. C	
12. C	27. B	42. D	
13. B	28. A	43. A	
14. D	29. C	44. B	
15. B	30. B	45. D	

TEST 5

DIRECTIONS: Each question or incomplete statement is followed by several suggested answers or completions. Select the one that BEST answers the question or completes the statement. *PRINT THE LETTER OF THE CORRECT ANSWER IN THE SPACE AT THE RIGHT.*

1. It is reasonable to expect that a Station Agent would be required to 1.______
   A. make minor repairs in the booth
   B. detain disorderly people
   C. make written reports of his activities
   D. operate trains in emergencies

2. It is simple logic that the reason every stairway in a subway station has a number is to 2.______
   A. guide passengers
   B. simplify reporting
   C. avoid duplication
   D. show which street it is near

3. The color of the signal used in the subway to show the train operator he has a clear track is 3.______
   A. red B. yellow C. blue D. green

4. The Coliseum is located at 4.______
   A. Times Square B. Grand Central
   C. Madison Square D. Columbus Circle

5. There is a subway station at Grand Central on the _______ Line. 5.______
   A. IND 6th Ave. B. BMT – Canarsie
   C. IRT Flushing D. IND Queens

6. The maps which are displayed at subway stations do NOT show 6.______
   A. how far it is from one station to the next
   B. which stations are express stops
   C. which lines are IND, BMT, or IRT
   D. where there are transfer points

7. A passenger asks for two fares and hands the Station Agent $5.00. If fares cost $2 each, the SMALLEST number of bills the passenger can be given in change is 7.______
   A. 0 B. 1 C. 2 D. 3

8. Station Agents are forbidden by the rules to allow any person to be in the booth except for certain designated employees of the railroad when on official business. A logical reason for this rule is that 8.______
   A. most booths are too small
   B. the presence of more than one person in a booth makes a poor impression on passengers
   C. money is handled in the booths
   D. it takes considerable concentration to sell tokens

Questions 9-16.

DIRECTIONS: Questions 9 through 16, inclusive, are based on the bulletin order shown below. Refer to this bulletin order when answering these questions.

BULLETIN ORDER NO. 9

Subject: Plugged Turnstiles *January 19, ...*

Station Agents, especially those assigned to the midnight tour of duty, are again warned to be alert when a passenger reports that his token is stuck in a turnstile which will not let him through. If no platformman or gateman is available, take the passenger's name and address without leaving the booth and request the passenger to pay an additional fare using one of the other turnstiles. Inform the passenger that the Authority will reimburse him for actual fare lost.

Station Agents are not to leave booths unattended in such instances, but will telephone the Station Department immediately.

Station Agents should notify the Transit Police Bureau immediately of any suspicious acts observed and are redirected to keep booth doors locked at all times. Booth doors must be closed and locked when Station Agents are taking turnstile readings or retrieving tokens.

John Doe,
Superintendent

9. When a passenger reports a stuck turnstile, the Station Agent should telephone the 9.______
   A. Superintendent B. Authority
   C. Transit Police Bureau D. Station Department

10. The TOTAL number of times that the title *Station Agents* appears in the entire bulletin is 10.______
    A. 3 B. 4 C. 5 D. 6

11. When a passenger reports that a Metrocard is stuck in a turnstile, the Station Agent should 11.______
    A. notify the Transit Police immediately
    B. tell the passenger to look for a gateman
    C. lock his booth and inspect the turnstile
    D. take the passenger's name and address

12. A passenger who properly reports the loss of a token in a plugged turnstile will PROBABLY be reimbursed through a(the) 12.______
A. special messenger
B. Station Agent
C. gateman
D. regular mail

13. Retrieving money, as used in this bulletin, MOST probably means 13.______
A. taking out fares which have been deposited in turnstiles
B. picking up fares which have dropped to the floor
C. paying out cash for fares returned by passengers
D. counting the number of fares sold since the previous count

14. If Station Agents at a certain location work in three consecutive 8-hour tours to cover the 24 hours in a day and the A.M. tour finished at 3:00 P.M., the hours of work for the midnight tour are MOST likely _______ to _______. 14.______
A. 12:00 midnight; 8:00 A.M.
B. 11:00 P.M.; 7:00 A.M.
C. 10:00 P.M.; 6:00 A.M.
D. 9:00 P.M.; 5:00 A.M.

15. If Bulletin Order No. 1 was issued on January 2, bulletins are being issued at the rate of 15.______
A. one a day
B. one a week
C. one every two days
D. two a week

16. From the statements in this bulletin, it is clear that there MUST be 16.______
A. gatemen on duty at every change booth
B. telephones in all change booths
C. suspicious characters around every station
D. platformmen always on duty

Questions 17-26.

DIRECTIONS: Questions 17 through 26, inclusive, in Column I are the names of well-known places in the city, each of which is situated in one of the five boroughs listed in Column II. For each name in Column I, select the borough in which it is situated from Column II.

COLUMN I	COLUMN II	
17. Rockaway Park	A. Bronx	17.______
18. Battery Park	B. Brooklyn	18.______
19. Gowanus Canal	C. Manhattan	19.______
20. Bush Terminal	D. Queens	20.______
21. Yankee Stadium	E. Richmond	21.______
22. United Nations Headquarters		22.______
23. Sheepshead Bay		23.______

24. Ferry Terminal at St. George 24.______

25. Forest Hills Tennis Stadium 25.______

26. Van Cortland Park 26.______

27. New York's Municipal Building is located NEAREST to 27.______
A. South Ferry B. Bowling Green
C. City Hall D. Canal Street

28. The name of the residence provided for New York's mayor is 28.______
A. Hamilton Grange B. Jumel Mansion
C. Dyckman House D. Gracie Mansion

29. Before Metrocards, one advantage of using two-dollar tokens for subway fare instead of requiring passengers to use regular coins that totaled two dollars was that 29.______
A. it was easier for passengers to insert one token than two or more coins
B. tokens were more difficult to counterfeit than coins
C. it made less work for the Station Agent
D. tokens were less likely to be lost than coins

Questions 30-39.

DIRECTIONS: Questions 30 through 39 refer to the arithmetic examples shown in the boxes below. Be sure to refer to the proper box when answering each question.

8462 2974 5109 763 47 BOX 1	$14\overline{)1890}$ BOX 2	182 x 63 BOX 3	27412 - 8426 BOX 4	$275.15 - 162.28 BOX 5
2/3 X 246 BOX 6	14.36 x 7.2 BOX 7	14.6 9.22 143.18 27.1 BOX 8	$6.45 ÷ $0.15 BOX 9	16.6 – 7.91 BOX 10

30. The sum of the five numbers in Box 1 is 30.______
A. 16245 B. 16355 C. 17245 D. 17355

31. The result of the division indicated in Box 2 is 31.______
A. 140 B. 135 C. 127 6/7 D. 125

32. The product of the two numbers in Box 3 is 32.______
A. 55692 B. 16552 C. 11466 D. 1638

33. The difference between the two numbers in Box 4 is 33.______
A. 18986 B. 19096 C. 35838 D. 38986

34. The difference between the two numbers in Box 5 is 34.______
A. $103.87 B. $112.87 C. $113.97 D. $212.87

35. The product of the two numbers in Box 6 is 35.______
A. 82 B. 123 C. 164 D. 369

36. The product of the two numbers in Box 7 is 36.______
A. 103.492 B. 103.392 C. 102.392 D. 102.292

37. The sum of the four numbers in Box 8 is 37.______
A. 183.00 B. 183.10 C. 194.10 D. 204.00

38. The result of the division indicated in Box 9 is 38.______
A. $0.43 B. 4.3 C. 43 D. $4.30

39. The difference between the two numbers in Box 10 is 39.______
A. 8.69 B. 8.11 C. 6.25 D. 3.75

Questions 40-46.

DIRECTIONS: Questions 40 through 46 are based on the Procedure for Inspections, Repairs, or Alterations to Low Turnstiles given below. Refer to this procedure when answering these questions.

PROCEDURE FOR INSPECTION, REPAIRS, OR ALTERATIONS TO LOW TURNSTILES

When a maintainer arrives at a station to repair or inspect a turnstile, the Station Agent and the maintainer together will take the register reading of the turnstile, and the Station Agent will record the reading on Form TAA-G-458 before any work is begun.

When the work is completed and before the turnstile is opened for service, the Station Agent and the maintainer together will again take the register reading. The Station Agent will enter this second reading on Form TAA-G-458. The difference between the two readings, representing the number of test registrations made on that turnstile, will also be entered.

The turnstile maintainer shall make a report in duplicate on Form TAM-L27 showing the register readings before and after adjustment, and shall have the Station Agent initial the readings as verification. If test operation is by observation of passengers entering through the turnstile just repaired, the number of such passengers shall be noted in the *Remarks* column. The turnstile maintainer shall also enter the time of start and finish of the work, and on the original copy of the report only, the type of inspection or work done.

The Station Agent shall transmit the duplicate of Form TAM-L27 together with his Form TAA-G-458 to Audit of Passenger Revenue.

40. The number of entries on the maintainer's Form TAM-L27 that the Station Agent is required to initial for each turnstile worked on is 40.______
A. 1 B. 2 C. 3 D. 4

41. The number of entries that the railroad clerk is required to make on Form TAA-G-458 is 41.______
A. 1 B. 2 C. 3 D. 4

42. In accordance with the foregoing, the number of copies of Form TAA-G-458 that MUST be made out by the Station Agent is 42.______
A. 4 B. 3 C. 2 D. 1

43. With respect to Form TAM-L27, the letters TA MOST likely stands for 43.______
A. transit authority B. token adjustment
C. turnstile alteration D. time account

44. The form of test operation specifically mentioned in the procedure is by 44.______
A. use of special counters
B. observation of passengers entering
C. use of a stated number of tokens
D. changing the register reading

45. It is stated in the procedure that the maintainer should enter in the *Remarks* column of Form TAM-L27 the 45.______
A. initial register reading
B. number of test registration
C. number of passengers involved in test registrations
D. final register reading

46. The information that is NOT included when the Station Agent transmits the two forms to Audit of Passenger Revenue is the 46.______
A. final turnstile reading
B. type of work done
C. number of test registrations
D. number of test operations made by passengers entering

47. If, while on duty, a Station Agent observed an accident involving passenger injuries, it would be MOST important for the Station Agent to first 47.______
A. render all possible first aid to the injured
B. telephone to headquarters for orders
C. record the time of day
D. write out an accident report

48. Of the following dates, the GREATEST number of passengers would be expected to use the subway in 2015 on 48.______
A. Monday, October 12 B. Friday, December 25
C. Sunday, May 24 D. Tuesday, October 13

49. The HEAVIEST weekday traffic on the subway occurs at 49.______
A. 8:30 A.M. B. 11:30 A.M. C. 7:30 P.M. D. 11:30 P.M.

50. Accidents to subway employees are MOST effectively prevented by 50.______
A. safety posters
B. expensive safety devices
C. alertness of employees
D. short working days

KEY (CORRECT ANSWERS)

1. C	16. B	31. B	46. B
2. B	17. D	32. C	47. A
3. D	18. C	33. A	48. D
4. D	19. B	34. B	49. A
5. C	20. B	35. C	50. C
6. A	21. A	36. B	
7. B	22. C	37. C	
8. C	23. B	38. C	
9. D	24. E	39. A	
10. B	25. D	40. B	
11. D	26. A	41. C	
12. D	27. C	42. D	
13. A	28. D	43. A	
14. B	29. A	44. B	
15. C	30. D	45. C	

EXAMINATION SECTION

TEST 1

DIRECTIONS: Each question or incomplete statement is followed by several suggested answers or completions. Select the one that BEST answers the question or completes the statement. *PRINT THE LETTER OF THE CORRECT ANSWER IN THE SPACE AT THE RIGHT.*

Questions 1-7.

DIRECTIONS: Questions 1 through 7 refer to the Tabulation of Turnstile Readings shown below and to the notes given beneath the tabulation. Refer to this tabulation and the notes in answering these questions.

TABULATION OF TURNSTILE READINGS

Turnstile Number	TURNSTILE READINGS AT					
	5:30 A.M.	6:00 A.M.	7:00 A.M.	8:00 A.M.	9:00 A.M.	10:00 A.M.
1	45863	45872	45992	46348	46619	46756
2	89768	89789	89902	90713	91237	91285
3	89987	90006	90197	91312	91927	92011
4	18956	18963	19058	19561	19951	20000

NOTES: 1. Turnstiles are operated by fares costing $2 each.
2. The subway entrance at which these turnstiles are located is open, with a Station Agent, from 5:30 A.M. to 10:00 A.M.

1. The number of passengers using turnstile No. 2 from 6:00 A.M. to 8:00 A.M. was 1.______
   A. 113 B. 713 C. 724 D. 924

2. The MOST used turnstile from opening to closing was No. 2.______
   A. 1 B. 2 C. 3 D. 4

3. The total number of passengers using turnstile No. 1 from opening to closing was 3.______
   A. 883 B. 893 C. 1883 D. 1893

4. From 8:00 A.M. to 9:00 A.M., the Station Agent sold exactly 800 fares, while the turnstile readings for the four turnstiles show that a total of 1800 passengers passed through them in the same period. 4.______
   The number of passengers who purchased fares was MOST probably
   A. *less* than 800 B. *exactly* 800
   C. *between* 800 and 1000 D. *exactly* 1800

5. The cash taken in for the 800 fares of Question 4 was 5.______
   A. $320 B. $800 C. $1200 D. $1600

6. The number of passengers using turnstile No. 3 in the first half hour was 6.______
A. 119 B. 81 C. 19 D. 9

7. The turnstile passing the FEWEST passengers from 9:00 A.M. to 10:00 A.M. was No. 7.______
A. 1 B. 2 C. 3 D. 4

8. Arranging the names Baker, Baketon, Bakewell, and Bakenny in alphabetical order, the THIRD name should be 8.______
A. Baker B. Bakenny C. Bakewell D. Baketon

9. According to the LATEST recommended first aid practice, a cut finger should be cleaned with 9.______
A. soap and water B. phenol
C. mercurochrome D. iodine

10. If a passenger called a Station Agent improper names but took no other action, the Station Agent would show good judgment by 10.______
A. calling the passenger names in return
B. holding the passenger while another passenger called the transit police
C. acting as if the passenger were not there
D. telling the passenger to keep his mouth shut

11. The official notice of this examination stated that candidates must be acceptable for bonding at the time of appointment. 11.______
The reason for this requirement is that the work of a Station Agent involves
A. reading turnstile registers
B. meeting the public
C. handling considerable money
D. keeping detailed records

12. If your supervisor tells you and another Station Agent to do something and you do not fully understand the order, it would be BEST for you to 12.______
A. discuss the order with the other Station Agent to decide what was meant
B. ask your supervisor to put the order in writing
C. keep quiet and use your own best judgment
D. ask your supervisor for a further explanation

13. The MOST important of the following reasons for prohibiting smoking in the subway is to 13.______
A. prevent spreading of germs
B. prevent burning passengers' clothes
C. keep the trains clean of butts
D. prevent damage to car floors

14. The MAIN reason that the edges of the top steps on many stairways in the subway are painted yellow is to 14.______
A. show up the dirt
B. make them less slippery
C. make them more attractive
D. make them stand out

15. Four different subway lines have stations named *Times Square*. Three of these lines are the 7th Avenue Line, the 42nd Street Shuttle and the Flushing Line. The fourth line is the _______ Line. 15._____
A. 8th Avenue B. 6th Avenue
C. Lexington Avenue D. Broadway

16. To change from Standard Time to Daylight Savings Time, the hands of the clock are moved 16._____
A. *ahead* in spring B. *ahead* in autumn
C. *back* in spring D. *back* in autumn

17. If a Station Agent finds two orders on his bulletin board giving conflicting orders with regard to his work, he should follow the one which is 17._____
A. dated later B. dated earlier
C. easier to carry out D. best in his judgment

18. Station Agents are required to keep their records on printed forms because 18._____
A. this prevents any errors
B. such forms require no ability
C. this prevents dishonesty
D. there are many clerks and they all do the same work

19. When the Station Agent is selling tokens, he should be CHIEFLY concerned with 19._____
A. safety B. accuracy C. speed D. courtesy

20. The borough in which there are NO subways operated by the city is 20._____
A. Bronx B. Queens C. Brooklyn D. Richmond

21. The Transit Authority permits the posting of advertisements in subway cars because 21._____
A. it promotes safety
B. passengers like to read the *ads*
C. it improves the interior appearance of the cars
D. advertisers pay for this privilege

22. A passenger tendered $2.10 in payment for a two-dollar fare and received one coin in change. 22._____
The change consisted of
A. one dime B. three nickels
C. a quarter and a nickel D. a quarter and a dime

23. When a Station Agent witnesses an accident while on duty, he must make a written report. 23._____
It is MOST important that such reports be
A. accurate as to facts B. brief
C. very detailed D. submitted immediately

24. If the first day of a 31-day month falls on a Thursday, the LAST day will fall on a 24._____
A. Wednesday B. Thursday C. Friday D. Saturday

25. A Station Agent will MOST likely check whether a half-dollar is counterfeit by 25.______
A. attempting to bend the coin
B. examining it under a magnifying glass
C. sounding the coin on a hard surface
D. testing it with his teeth

26. The legislative body which makes the local law in the city is the 26.______
A. Board of Aldermen B. City Council
C. Board of Supervisors D. City Assembly

27. One subway line which does NOT run north and south anywhere in Manhattan is the 27.______
A. Broadway Line B. 42nd Street Shuttle
C. 8th Avenue Line D. Lexington Line

Questions 28-35.

DIRECTIONS: Questions 28 through 35 are based on the portion of the Arrival Timetable for Bay St. local station of the subway shown below. This table shows the times when trains are scheduled to arrive at Bay St. Station. Refer to this timetable, and consider only the period of time covered by the table when answering these questions.

ARRIVAL TIMETABLE

SOUTHBOUND				NORTHBOUND			
Col. 1	Col. 2	Col. 3	Col. 4	Col. 5	Col. 6	Col. 7	Col. 8
Mon. PM to Fri. AM	Fri. PM to Sat. AM	Sat. PM to Sun. AM	Sun. PM to Mon. AM	Mon. PM to Fri. AM	Fri. PM to Sat. AM	Sat. PM to Sun. AM	Sun. PM to Mon. AM
11:42	11:42	11:42	11:44	11:44	11:44	11:25	11:44
11:54	11:52	11:52	11:54	11:54	11:54	11:33	11:54
12:06	12:02	12:02	12:06	12:04	12:04	11:41	12:04
12:18	12:12	12:12	12:18	12:14	12:14	11:49	12:14
12:30	12:22	12:22	12:30	12:24	12:24	11:57	12:24
12:42	12:34	12:32	12:42	12:34	12:34	12:05	12:34
12:54	12:46	12:42	12:54	12:46	12:44	12:15	12:46
1:09	12:58	12:52	1:09	12:58	12:54	12:25	12:58
1:24	1:13	1:02	1:24	1:10	1:04	12:35	1:10
1:44	1:28	1:14	1:44	1:22	1:14	12:45	1:22
2:04	1:41	1:26	2:04	1:34	1:24	12:55	1:34
2:24	1:56	1:38	2:24	1:46	1:34	1:05	1:46

28. Two columns which show exactly the same arrival for every train are 28.______
A. 1 and 3 B. 2 and 4 C. 5 and 8 D. 6 and 7

29. The number of nights per week to which Column 1 applies is 29.______
A. 5 B. 4 C. 3 D. 1

30. The total number of northbound trains scheduled to arrive at Bay St. Station from 12:45 A.M. to 1:15 A.M. on Tuesday is 30.______
A. 5 B. 3 C. 2 D. 1

31. The total number of all trains scheduled to arrive at this station between 11:45 P.M. Friday and 1:30 A.M. Saturday is 31.______
A. 9 B. 10 C. 19 D. 21

32. A northbound train is due at this station at 12:34 A.M. every day of the week EXCEPT 32.______
A. Friday B. Saturday C. Sunday D. Monday

33. A passenger who wants to get a northbound train anytime after 11:59 P.M. on Wednesday can tell from the timetable that the MAXIMUM length of time he must wait for the next train if he just misses one is ______ minutes. 33.______
A. 15 B. 12 C. 10 D. 8

34. The total time elapsed from the first to the last train of Column 6 is 34.______
A. 2 hrs., 10 min. B. 150 min.
C. 1 hr., 50 min. D. 1 hr., 10 min.

35. If a passenger who wishes to board a southbound train arrives on Bay St. platform at midnight on Saturday, he can expect to board a train at 35.______
A. 12:06 B. 12:05 C. 12:04 D. 12:02

36. A thorough knowledge of the Transit Authority's printed rules and regulations will MOST likely help a Station Agent to know 36.______
A. when he may leave his booth during his tour of duty
B. where points of interest are located near his booth
C. when to expect vandalism near his booth
D. how to travel from home to his booth

37. If a Station Agent has to telephone for an ambulance for an injured person, the MOST important information he must transmit is 37.______
A. where the ambulance is needed
B. the name of the injured person
C. how the accident occurred
D. what part of the body has been injured

38. When an ambulance arrives at a subway station to take away an unconscious person, it would probably be MOST difficult for the Station Agent to obtain the name of the 38.______
A. station B. ambulance attendant
C. hospital D. injured person

39. The official rules limit the size of newspaper bundles which a newspaper carrier may take into the subway because bundles of unrestricted size would be 39.______
A. more likely to interfere with passengers
B. difficult to get through the gates
C. too heavy for the carrier
D. difficult to tie securely

40. The PRINCIPAL duty of a Station Agent who is assigned to a change booth is to 40.______
A. catch cheaters B. give directions
C. prevent vandalism D. sell fares

41. On checking a pile of tickets arranged in numerical order, you find that the next ticket after number 21,986 is number 22,008. 41.______
The number of tickets missing is
A. 11 B. 12 C. 21 D. 32

42. Employees MUST know the rules and regulations governing their jobs so that they may 42.______
A. justify mistakes
B. foresee all emergencies
C. avoid antagonizing their superiors
D. perform their duties properly

43. In accordance with generally recommended good telephone answering practice, Robert Gray stationed in Booth 202 at 40th Street Station on the Crosstown Line would BEST answer the telephone by saying, 43.______
A. "40th Street, Booth 202, Gray speaking"
B. "Crosstown, Booth 202. Who's calling?"
C. "Gray speaking"
D. "This is 40th Street. Who do you want?"

44. The BEST way for the average regular subway passenger to avoid long waits in line to buy fares is to buy them 44.______
A. in batches of 6 to 10 at a time when leaving the subway
B. two at a time when entering the subway
C. in batches of 6 to 10 at a time when entering the subway
D. two at a time when leaving the subway

45. Telephones of the transit system are reserved for official business. 45.______
The type of call which should receive preference because of its importance in maintaining service is one pertaining to
A. an employee reporting for duty
B. details of a work schedule
C. movement of trains
D. ordering of new material

46. Station Agents are not permitted to use the transit system telephones for making personal calls MAINLY because such calls would 46.______
A. never be justified
B. require additional records
C. interfere with incoming business calls
D. cause arguments

47. If a passenger tells a Station Agent that he lost an umbrella in the subway on the preceding day, the passenger should be advised to inquire about it at the 47.______
A. porter's room
B. Transit Authority Lost Property Office
C. newsstand
D. local police headquarters

48. Standard forms frequently call for entries on them to be printed because printing, as compared to writing, is GENERALLY 48.______
A. easier to do
B. more legible
C. more legal
D. more compact

49. The first aid procedure of not moving a person unless absolutely necessary is MOST important in the case of a person who has 49.______
A. fainted
B. collapsed from the heat
C. fractured his leg
D. broken a finger

50. It would be MOST important to question in detail a person who turns in as found a 50.______
A. basket of fruit
B. five-dollar bill
C. gold ring
D. revolver

KEY (CORRECT ANSWERS)

1. D	16. A	31. C	46. C
2. C	17. A	32. C	47. B
3. B	18. D	33. B	48. B
4. A	19. B	34. C	49. C
5. D	20. D	35. D	50. D
6. C	21. D	36. A	
7. B	22. A	37. A	
8. D	23. A	38. D	
9. A	24. D	39. A	
10. C	25. C	40. D	
11. C	26. B	41. C	
12. D	27. B	42. D	
13. B	28. C	43. A	
14. D	29. B	44. A	
15. D	30. B	45. C	

TEST 2

DIRECTIONS: Each question or incomplete statement is followed by several suggested answers or completions. Select the one that BEST answers the question or completes the statement. *PRINT THE LETTER OF THE CORRECT ANSWER IN THE SPACE AT THE RIGHT.*

1. If it becomes necessary to eject a disorderly person from the TA's property, FIRST consideration by the employees should be given the 1.______
   A. effect it may have on the riding public
   B. protection of transit property
   C. safety of fellow employees
   D. safety of passengers

2. Discontent with working conditions on the part of Station Agents can be MOST effectively minimized if their superiors 2.______
   A. exercise intelligent supervision
   B. grant overtime whenever asked
   C. favor the senior employees
   D. overlook minor infractions of rules

3. If it necessary for a Station Agent to enter upon the tracks, he should expect trains to 3.______
   A. approach from either direction
   B. always operate in direction of traffic
   C. travel faster at night than in daytime
   D. always be on schedule

4. Bellevue Hospital is located NEAREST to 4.______
   A. South Ferry B. Radio City
   C. City Hall D. Stuyvesant Square

5. A Station Agent at a busy station is LEAST apt to run out of 5.______
   A. tokens B. nickels C. dimes D. quarters

6. Station Agents are NOT required to change bills larger than ten dollars. A GOOD reason for this ruling is that 6.______
   A. larger bills may be counterfeit
   B. to do so would take too much time
   C. the loss would be greater if a large bill were lost
   D. small bills are more common

7. Absences on the part of Station Agents are most objectionable, and notices of intention to be absent from work most essential, where the Station Agent involved is assigned to a full-time booth rather than a part-time booth because 7.______
   A. full-time booths are located in busy stations
   B. a substitute must be provided
   C. part-time booths need less experienced Station Agents
   D. the duties are essentially different in these booths

8. In cases of stolen reduced fare tickets, information relative to the subsequent disposal of these tickets may MOST likely be obtained by 8.______
A. changing the color of subsequently issued tickets
B. interrogating the custodian of the tickets
C. alerting Station Agents on the thefts
D. refusing further tickets to students of the school concerned

9. To be able to give the correct travel directions to the public regarding a certain bus line, it is LEAST essential for a Station Agent to know that bus line's 9.______
A. route B. terminals
C. headway D. transfer privileges

10. Station Agents are required to promptly report the closing of a defective turnstile. The reason for a prompt report is to 10.______
A. fix responsibility
B. permit provision for quick repairs
C. determine if the turnstile is really needed
D. prevent loss of revenue

11. Greenwich Village is located in 11.______
A. Manhattan B. the Bronx C. Brooklyn D. Queens

12. The total amount of revenue (in bills and currency) turned in by a Station Agent at the end of his tour will depend DIRECTLY on the 12.______
A. tour he has worked
B. number of people entering the turnstiles
C. number of tokens sold
D. location of his station

13. Of the following, the BEST way to have transit employees, as a whole, learn good safety habits is to 13.______
A. penalize them with loss of pay for lost-time accidents
B. have them read the rules in their spare time
C. offer prizes for the best safety records
D. let them learn through their own mistakes

14. Specific air-raid test instructions should be followed by all personnel to 14.______
A. test the employees' ability to follow instructions
B. improve the instructions
C. assure cooperation
D. minimize disorder

15. A passenger may recover a lost article which has been found and turned over to the lost and found department by 15.______
A. proving undisputed title to it
B. properly identifying it
C. paying the storage charges
D. simply asking for it

Questions 16-23.

DIRECTIONS: Questions 16 through 23 in Column I are questions of simple arithmetic, each of which has one of the answers listed in Column II. For each item in Column I, select the CORRECT answer from Column II.

	COLUMN I	COLUMN II	
16.	229 times 9	A. 1383	16.______
17.	11064 divided by 8	B. 1752	17.______
18.	1384 plus 368	C. 2061	18.______
19.	3021 minus 447 minus 386	D. 2682	19.______
20.	149 times 3 times 6	E. 2188	20.______
21.	727 plus 17 plus 639		21.______
22.	2881 minus 693		22.______
23.	43281 divided by 3 divided by 7		23.______

24. The Brooklyn Bridge Station of the Lexington Ave. Line is located NEAREST to 24.______
A. City Hall
B. Brooklyn Borough Hall
C. the Custom House
D. the Navy Yard

25. Under Civil Service, appointments depend PRIMARILY on 25.______
A. experience
B. physical fitness
C. record and seniority
D. the outcome of competitive examinations

26. The TA has its main office at 26.______
A. 370 Jay Street, Brooklyn
B. 73 Rockwell Place, Brooklyn
C. 299 Broadway, Manhattan
D. 126 W. 53rd Street, Manhattan

27. Transfers on the subway system are issued MAINLY for the benefit of the 27.______
A. employees
B. supervisory force
C. passengers
D. firms printing them

28. If you are assigned to a station used by several lines and a passenger asks you how to reach a certain destination with which you are not acquainted, the BEST procedure would be to 28.______
    A. use your best judgment
    B. admit you do not know
    C. tell him to take the first train in and consult the map in the car
    D. advise him to look up a policeman

29. The MAXIMUM number of tokens that could be purchased with six dollars is 29.______
    A. 3 B. 6 C. 7 D. 8

30. The number of paying passengers entering the subway at any station is given DIRECTLY by 30.______
    A. the turnstile meter readings
    B. the amount of revenue collected
    C. a platform man using a mechanical counter
    D. a tally kept by the railroad clerk

31. Columbus Circle is located NEAREST to the 31.______
    A. Lincoln Tunnel B. Hayden Planetarium
    C. Empire State Building D. Madison Square Garden

32. A Station Agent making change should always be on the alert for counterfeit bills. The counterfeit bill will USUALLY differ from the genuine in the 32.______
    A. size of the bill B. width of the margin
    C. condition of the paper D. clarity of the portrait

33. By common sense, you would expect an oncoming train to stop if you moved a lantern 33.______
    A. in a circle over your head
    B. to and fro along the track
    C. straight up and down
    D. back and forth across the track

34. The subway line which has a station NEAREST to Queensboro Bridge Plaza is the 34.______
    A. 4th Avenue Line
    B. Lexington Avenue Line
    C. 6th Avenue Line
    D. 8th Avenue Line

35. Many subway change booths are NOT open at night because 35.______
    A. most Station Agents do not like night work
    B. only a small number of people travel at night
    C. fewer trains operate at night
    D. there is less possibility of error when making change in daylight

36. Safety programs are conducted throughout the transit system. 36.______
The MAIN purpose of these programs is to
A. eliminate accidents
B. encourage cooperation among employees
C. improve system efficiency
D. produce a faster schedule

37. A bulletin order will USUALLY be superseded by another bulletin order where 37.______
A. a copy of the original order has been lost
B. the original order has been in force a long time
C. a change has been made in the procedure described in the original order
D. the person issuing the original order has been replaced by another

38. Occasionally, a United States Post Office makes arrangements with the Transit Authority for the prepayment of fares whereby letter carriers attached to that post office are not required to pay a fare when on duty. 38.______
This kind of agreement is desirable MAINLY because it
A. eliminates counting of extra fares
B. permits the letter carrier to carry more mail
C. increases the total number of passengers using the subway
D. minimizes congestion at the turnstiles

Questions 39-42.

DIRECTIONS: Questions 39 through 42 are based on the regulations relating to voting on Primary Day as given below. Read these regulations carefully before answering these questions.

REGULATIONS RELATING TO VOTING ON PRIMARY DAY

The polls are open from 3:00 to 10:00 P.M. Employees who are on duty Primary Day during the period polls are open and who would not have two consecutive hours free time to vote will be granted leave of absence for two hours without loss of pay.

Examples:
1. Employees reporting for work at 3 P.M. to and including 4:59 P.M. will be allowed two hours leave with pay.
2. Employees who report to work at 5 P.M. or thereafter, no time to be allowed.
3. Employees who complete their tour of duty and are cleared on or before 8 P.M., no time to be allowed.

39. A two-hours' leave of absence with pay will be granted to employees who are on duty Primary Day if they 39.______
A. have to work two hours while the polls are open
B. would not have two consecutive hours free time to vote
C. are working a day tour
D. are working a night tour

40. An employee working an evening tour will be allowed two hours with pay if he has to report for work at 40.______
A. 3:00 P.M. B. 5:00 P.M. C. 7:00 P.M. D. 9:00 P.M.

41. An employee working an afternoon tour will be allowed two hours with pay if he clears at 41.______
A. 6:00 P.M. B. 7:00 P.M. C. 8:00 P.M. D. 9:00 P.M.

42. An employee working an afternoon tour will NOT be allowed any time off if he clears at 42.______
A. 8:00 P.M. B. 8:30 P.M. C. 9:30 P.M. D. 10:00 P.M.

43. Radio City is located NEAREST to 43.______
A. Union Square B. Pennsylvania Station
C. Times Square D. Hudson Terminal

44. Elementary School Tickets as issued are valid for one month only. 44.______
The means used to quickly diminish a new ticket from one which has just expired is to
A. use bolder type in printing the ticket
B. increase the size of the ticket
C. change the color of the ticket
D. recall all expired tickets before issuing new ones

45. A passenger tendered a Station Agent fifteen dollars and received seven fares, one nickel, two dimes, and two quarters. 45.______
In this case, the Station Agent gave the passenger
A. twenty-five cents too little
B. five cents too much
C. ten cents too little
D. ten cents too much

46. Many transit lines use Metrocards for their turnstiles. 46.______
One advantage in using Metrocards is that
A. the revenue increases when Metrocards are used
B. daily receipts of a booth are more readily calculated if Metrocards are used
C. an increase in fare will not require a change in turnstiles
D. the loss to the line is less if a passenger loses a Metrocard than if he loses a coin

47. In a certain station, if the revenue receipts for the second tour were twice as great as for the first tour, and six times as great for the third tour as for the first tour, it follows that the receipts for the third tour were _______ as great as for the second tour. 47.______
A. three times B. twice C. one-half D. one-third

48. The subway line which has a station nearest to the Hall of Fame for Great Americans is the 48.______
A. Lexington Avenue Line
B. Broadway—7th Avenue Line
C. 6th Avenue Line
D. 8th Avenue Line

49. If a change in the handling of returned lost property is to be made, the BEST way to notify Station Agents of the change is by 49.______
   A. personal contacts by assistant station supervisors
   B. an individual notice to each Station Agent
   C. notifying Station Agents on the day tour and having them inform the other Station Agents
   D. means of bulletin orders

50. A Station Agent should be LEAST concerned if a passenger tells him that 50.______
   A. a vending machine was broken into
   B. the trains on the lower level are running behind schedule
   C. there was a puddle of oil on the station platform
   D. a bundle of newspapers was lying on the edge of a station platform

KEY (CORRECT ANSWERS)

1. D	16. C	31. D	46. C
2. A	17. A	32. D	47. A
3. A	18. B	33. D	48. A
4. D	19. E	34. A	49. D
5. A	20. D	35. B	50. B
6. B	21. A	36. A	
7. B	22. E	37. C	
8. C	23. C	38. D	
9. C	24. A	39. B	
10. B	25. D	40. A	
11. A	26. A	41. D	
12. C	27. B	42. A	
13. C	28. C	43. C	
14. D	29. A	44. C	
15. B	30. A	45. A	

TEST 3

DIRECTIONS: Each question or incomplete statement is followed by several suggested answers or completions. Select the one that BEST answers the question or completes the statement. *PRINT THE LETTER OF THE CORRECT ANSWER IN THE SPACE AT THE RIGHT.*

QUESTIONS 1-8.

DIRECTIONS: Questions 1 through 8 are based on the regulations governing Newspaper Carriers when on subway trains or station platforms. These Newspaper Carriers are issued badges which entitle them to enter subway stations, when carrying papers in accordance with these regulations, without paying a fare.

REGULATIONS GOVERNING NEWSPAPER CARRIERS
WHEN ON SUBWAY TRAINS OR STATION PLATFORMS

1. Carriers must wear badges at all times when on trains.
2. Carriers must not sort, separate, or wrap bundles on trains or insert sections.
3. Carriers must not obstruct platform of cars or stations.
4. Carriers may make delivery to stands inside the stations by depositing their badge with the station agent.
5. Throwing of bundles is strictly prohibited and will be cause for arrest.
6. Each bundle must not be over 18" x 12" x 15".
7. Not more than two bundles shall be carried by each carrier. (An extra fare to be charged for a second bundle.)
8. No wire to be used on bundles carried into stations.

1. These regulations do NOT prohibit carriers on trains from _______ newspapers. 1._______
   A. sorting bundles of
   B. carrying bundles of
   C. wrapping bundles of
   D. inserting sections into

2. A carrier delivering newspapers to a stand inside of the station MUST 2._______
   A. wear his badge at all times
   B. leave his badge with the Station Agent
   C. show his badge to the Station Agent
   D. show his badge at the newsstand

3. Carriers are warned against throwing bundles of newspapers from trains MAINLY because these acts may 3._______
   A. wreck the stand
   B. cause injury to passengers
   C. hurt the carrier
   D. damage the newspaper

4. It is permissible for a carrier to temporarily leave his bundles of newspapers 4.______
   A. near the subway car's door
   B. at the foot of the station stairs
   C. in front of the exit gate
   D. on a station bench

5. Of the following, the carrier who should NOT be restricted from entering the subway is the one carrying a bundle which is _______ long, _______ wide, and _______ high. 5.______
   A. 15"; 18"; 18" B. 18"; 12"; 18"
   C. 18"; 12"; 15" D. 18"; 15"; 15"

6. A carrier who will have to pay one fare is carrying _____ bundle(s). 6.______
   A. one B. two C. three D. four

7. Wire may NOT be used or tying bundles because it may be 7.______
   A. rusty
   B. expensive
   C. needed for other purposes
   D. dangerous to other passengers

8. If a carrier is arrested in violation of these regulations, the PROBABLE reason is that he 8.______
   A. carried too many papers
   B. was not wearing his badge
   C. separated bundles of newspapers on the train
   D. tossed a bundle of newspapers to a carrier on a train

Questions 9-22.

DIRECTIONS: Questions 9 through 22 are based on the portion of the employees' time sheet shown on the following page. When answering these questions, refer to this time sheet and the accompanying explanatory note. It contains all of the essential information required to determine the amount earned by each employee, and enough computations are made to show you the method for filling in the blank spaces in the time sheet. For your own convenience, you are advised to compute and fill in the blank spaces in your test before answering any of these items. Then answer each of the questions in the usual way.

EMPLOYEES' TIME SHEET

	Pay No.	Name	Hourly Rate	Time Reporting			Time Leaving			Time		Pay due
				Date	AM	PM	Date	AM	PM	Actually Worked	Overtime Credit	
REGULAR TIME	41	King	$7.80	2-2	7:00		2-2		3:00	8 hrs.	X	62.40
	39	Lee	7.20	2-2		11:00	2-3	7:00			X	
	85	Mark	8.10	2-3	7:00		2-3		3:00		X	
	64	Narr	7.50	2-3		3:00	2-3		11:00		X	
	75	Orr	7.20	2-4		3:00	2-4		11:00		X	
	29	Peer	8.10	2-5	7:00		2-5		3:00		X	
	36	Ray	7.80	2-5		11:00	2-6	7:00			X	
	45	Sill	7.80	2-6	7:00		2-6		3:00		X	
	91	Tone	7.20	2-6		3:00	2-6		11:00		X	
OVERTIME	41	King	7.80	2-2		3:00	2-2		5:00	2 hrs.	3 hrs.	23.40
	39	Lee	7.20	2-3	7:00		2-3	8:20				
	85	Mark	8.10	2-3		3:00	2-3		3:40			
	64	Narr	7.50	2-3		11:00	2-3		11:40			
	75	Orr	7.20	2-4		11:00	2-5	12:20				
	29	Peer	8.10	2-5		3:00	2-5		3:20			
	36	Ray	7.80	2-6	7:00		2-6	8:00				
	45	Sill	7.80	2-6		3:00	2-6		4:20			
	91	Tone	7.20	2-6		11:00	2-7	12:40				

NOTE: All overtime credit is at the rate of time and one-half.

9. On February 3, Mark should be credited for both regular time and overtime with a total of _______ hours, _______ minutes. 9._____
   A. 8; 40
   B. 9; 00
   C. 9; 20
   D. 9; 40

10. The individuals listed on the time sheet are designated by 10._____
    A. pay numbers
    B. hourly rates
    C. overtime rates
    D. dates

11. The difference between the maximum and the minimum hourly rates of pay as shown in the table is 11._____
    A. 30¢
    B. 60¢
    C. 90¢
    D. $1.20

12. The man earning the LARGEST amount for overtime (of the following) was 12._____
    A. Sill
    B. Tone
    C. Lee
    D. Orr

13. The man who earned $8.10 for overtime was 13._____
    A. Narr
    B. Mark
    C. Orr
    D. Ray

14. The number of men entitled to less than 9 hours pay was 14._____
    A. one
    B. two
    C. three
    D. four

15. Of the following, the man who put in the LEAST overtime was 15.______
A. Lee B. King C. Narr D. Orr

16. The two men earning the SMALLEST amount for overtime were 16.______
A. Narr and Peer
B. Narr and Mark
C. Mark and Ray
D. Ray and Peer

17. The table shows that more men were needed for overtime at _______ than at _______. 17.______
A. 7:00 A.M.; 3:00 P.M.
B. 7:00 A.M.; 11:00 P.M.
C. 11:00 P.M.; 3:00 A.M.
D. 11:00 P.M.; 7:00 A.M.

18. If Peer's overtime was due to the late arrival of his relief, who is paid at the hourly rate of $7.20, then the extra cost to the Transit Authority was 18.______
A. 45¢ B. 55¢ C. 90¢ D. $1.65

19. On February 3, the man earning the LARGEST amount for overtime was 19.______
A. Lee B. Mark C. Narr D. Orr

20. On February 6, Sill's pay for overtime was _______ of his total earnings. 20.______
A. 15% B. 20% C. 25% D. 30%

21. On February 6, Ray received a total pay of 21.______
A. $62.40 B. $66.30 C. $70.20 D. $74.10

22. On February 3, the total cost for overtime was 22.______
A. $15.60 B. $21.90 C. $22.50 D. $30.00

23. Queens College is located NEAREST to 23.______
A. Queens Plaza
B. LaGuardia Airport
C. Flushing Meadow Park
D. Kennedy Airport

24. The BASIC reason why unauthorized persons must be prevented from entering change booths is that the booths 24.______
A. contain money
B. are too small
C. contain system telephones
D. are not conveniently located

25. It is MOST NEARLY correct to say that 25.______
A. a careful employee never has an accident
B. accidents usually result from carelessness
C. careful supervision will eliminate all accidents
D. employees who study the rules carefully will not have an accident

26. A Station Agent in the course of his duties will be benefited MOST by a 26.______
A. tour of duty near his home
B. spacious change booth
C. large supply of tokens on hand
D. well-lighted change board

27. The subway line which has a station NEAREST to Grand Central Terminal is the _______ Line. 27.______
A. 6th Avenue
B. Broadway
C. Broadway—7th Avenue
D. Lexington Ave.

28. Station Agents should 28.______
A. detain suspicious characters
B. count the number of people entering the turnstiles
C. be on the alert for persons loitering near change booths
D. observe the type of people using the subway

29. The Atlantic Terminal of the LIRR is located NEAREST to the 29.______
A. Kings County Hospital
B. Brooklyn Navy Yard
C. Brooklyn Borough Hall
D. Barclays Center

30. A Station Agent would notify his superior rather than another employee if 30.______
A. he has no daily report form in the booth
B. a passenger complains about the service
C. he notices some water spilled on the station platform
D. the booth is very untidy

31. When using the system telephone, a Station Agent should make his conversation as brief as possible to avoid 31.______
A. errors when making change while talking
B. losing interest in his work
C. boring the listener
D. tying up the line

32. Bulletin orders pertaining to some subject matter are often reissued. The reason for this practice is that 32.______
A. other subject matter is not then available
B. the bulletins will then be read by the employees
C. the subject matter is considered extremely important
D. the original issue was lost

33. Bowling Green is located NEAREST to _______ Park. 33.______
A. Central
B. City Hall
C. Flushing Meadow
D. Marine

34. If a train operator in a subway train wishes to convey information to the Station Agent, he does so by 34.______
A. dashing over to the change booth
B. means of the train's whistle
C. asking a passenger to convey the message
D. dispatching the conductor to talk to the Station Agent

35. A bulletin order intended especially for Station Agents will NOT usually contain the 35.______
A. date of issue
B. name of superior by whom issued
C. time of day when it was issued
D. identifying bulletin order number

36. The subway line which has a station NEAREST to Brooklyn Borough Hall is the _______ Line. 36.______
A. Broadway—7th Avenue
B. Fulton Street
C. Broadway
D. 14th Street—Canarsie

37. If a Station Agent is slow in selling tokens, the MOST likely result will be 37.______
A. passengers will use other means of transportation
B. errors in making change
C. a line-up of people at the booth
D. a delay in schedules

38. Station Agents in MOST cases are assigned where they work alone. 38.______
This procedure is
A. due to the nature of their work
B. used to avoid unnecessary talking among employees
C. necessary to fix responsibility for revenue shortages
D. followed because the change booths are so small

39. The passenger who would NOT receive any coin in change is one who handed a Station Agent (fares are $2 each) 39.______
A. 8 dimes and 5 quarters and asked for 1 fare
B. 8 quarters and asked for 1 fare
C. 2 dollars, 1 dime, and asked for 1 fare
D. four dollars and a half dollar and asked for 2 fares

40. Metrocards should be well designed to 40.______
A. make them attractive to the users
B. minimize complaints by users
C. sell more of them
D. eliminate counterfeits

41. At a subway station located in a manufacturing district, the turnstile readings would MOST likely show the greatest number of passengers entering the station between the hours of _______ and _______. 41.______
A. 12 noon; 2:00 P.M.
B. 2:00 P.M.; 4:00 P.M.
C. 4:00 P.M.; 6:00 P.M.
D. 6:00 P.M.; 8:00 P.M.

42. In general, written orders are preferable to orders given orally because written orders 42.______
A. may be reviewed frequently
B. can go into detail more easily than verbal orders
C. can be immediately explained if not understood
D. are more easily complied with

43. At times it is necessary for an employee at the scene to quickly remove third rail power from the track. This can be done by means of emergency switch boxes provided along the tracks. 43.______
One logical reason for operating the emergency box would be
A. a fire on the track
B. to save power at night
C. to signal a train operator
D. to prevent a train from hitting a trackwalker

44. Safety rules are MOST useful because they 44.______
A. make it unnecessary to think
B. are a guide to avoid common dangers
C. prevent carelessness
D. fix responsibility for accidents

45. Of the following subway lines, the one which has a station NEAREST to Yankee Stadium is _______ Line. 45.______
A. Broadway—7th Avenue
B. Lexington Avenue
C. 8th Avenue
D. 6th Avenue

46. Accidents in the subway occur MOST frequently when the passengers are 46.______
A. passing through the turnstiles
B. walking on station platforms
C. using station stairways
D. crossing the subway tracks

47. In connection with accidents, it would be CORRECT to say that 47.______
A. accidents in dangerous work are excusable
B. every accident is the result of carelessness
C. serious accidents can never be anticipated
D. many safety rules are based on experience with past accidents

48. Van Cortlandt Park is located NEAREST to 48.______
A. Parkchester
B. Manhattan College
C. Fordham University
D. the Hall of Fame

49. As a newly appointed Station Agent, your assistant supervisor will MOST likely expect you to 49.______
A. make many mistakes
B. pay close attention to instructions
C. do your work better than the older Station Agents
D. work outside of your title

50. A Station Agent can MOST readily familiarize himself with new regulations by 50.______
A. reading all bulletins as they are issued
B. studying the book of rules
C. talking to other employees
D. questioning members of the supervisory force

8.(#3)

KEY (CORRECT ANSWERS)

1. B	16. A	31. D	46. C
2. B	17. D	32. C	47. D
3. B	18. D	33. B	48. B
4. D	19. A	34. B	49. B
5. C	20. B	35. C	50. A
6. A	21. D	36. A	
7. D	22. D	37. C	
8. D	23. C	38. B	
9. B	24. A	39. B	
10. A	25. B	40. B	
11. C	26. D	41. C	
12. B	27. D	42. A	
13. B	28. C	43. A	
14. A	29. D	44. B	
15. C	30. A	45. D	

TEST 4

DIRECTIONS: Each question or incomplete statement is followed by several suggested answers or completions. Select the one that BEST answers the question or completes the statement. *PRINT THE LETTER OF THE CORRECT ANSWER IN THE SPACE AT THE RIGHT.*

1. In dealing with passengers who appear at the booth, a Station Agent is BEST guided by the belief that 1.______
   A. most passengers have a chip on their shoulder
   B. most people respond to a pleasant reply
   C. passengers often ask silly questions
   D. the less said the better

2. A Station Agent must telephone notice of his intention to be absent from work at least two hours before his regular reporting time. 2.______
   The MOST likely reason for this is to
   A. avoid disrupting existing work schedules
   B. receive important instructions if any were issued
   C. permit his superior to question him
   D. permit proper action to cover his tour of duty

3. It is essential that a Station Agent on duty in a subway change booth be alerted if 3.______
   A. the supervisor is on his way to inspect the booth
   B. he is running low on supplies
   C. some reduced fare tickets had been stolen
   D. some trains are running behind schedule

4. The subway line which has a station NEAREST to City Hall is the _______ Division. 4.______
   A. 7th Avenue Line, IRT
   B. Sea Beach Express, BMT
   C. Brighton Beach Local Line, BMT
   D. *A* Line, IND

5. A number of air raid sirens are placed on the subway elevated structure and are operated by Station Agents. The Station Agent is used for this purpose rather than other subway employees because the Station Agent 5.______
   A. receives lower pay
   B. is on duty at the fixed location
   C. has more time
   D. is then better able to direct passengers

6. A Station Agent sees a passenger, apparently ill, fall to the floor some distance from his booth during a quiet period. 6.______
The Station Agent should
   A. immediately close the booth and go to the passenger
   B. not leave the booth since a holdup may be planned
   C. remain in the booth and call the nearest hospital
   D. send the next passenger to the person's assistance

7. If a passenger who has just received change goes some distance from the booth and then returns stating that he was short-changed a nickel, the Station Agent should 7.______
   A. tell him to return the next day when any overage will be known
   B. give him the nickel if he is sufficiently argumentative
   C. tell him to write a letter to the Board of Transportation
   D. inform him that change must be counted when received

8. Station Agents are not allowed to make statements concerning transit accidents except to other employees of the Board of Transportation in the regular course of business. 8.______
The PROBABLE reason for this rule is to
   A. prevent lawsuits
   B. conceal facts which may be damaging
   C. avoid conflicting testimony
   D. prevent unofficial statements from being accepted as official

9. The GREATEST advantage in the use of tokens is that 9.______
   A. it is difficult for passengers to insert two or more coins in turnstile slots
   B. counterfeits are less likely
   C. there will be less work for the railroad clerk
   D. the city will profit if tokens are lost

10. Bryant Park is located NEAREST to 10.______
   A. Grand Central Station
   B. Pennsylvania Railroad Station
   C. Columbus Circle
   D. The General Post Office

11. Transfer tickets for use between certain bus lines and the subway system have their color changed each day. 11.______
The MOST reasonable explanation for the change of color is to
   A. distinguish the tickets from regular transfers
   B. prevent the accidental sale of old tickets
   C. make it easier to detect the submission of old tickets
   D. prevent the use of stolen tickets

12. The TA rules limit the size of newspaper bundles which a newspaper carrier using his badge may carry into the subway because bundles of unrestricted size would be
    A. difficult to tie securely
    B. too heavy for the carrier
    C. more likely to interfere with passengers
    D. difficult to get through the turnstiles

12.______

13. Station Agents are required to take periodic readings of the turnstile passenger counter.
    If a Station Agent makes frequent errors in these readings, the LEAST likely cause is
    A. carelessness
    B. too much of a hurry
    C. poor lighting
    D. inexperience in taking readings

13.______

14. Some Station Agents have a habit of giving out change in two installments with an appreciable interval between.
    The PRINCIPAL objection to this procedure is that the
    A. passenger is more likely to drop the change
    B. passenger may judge it as a short change attempt
    C. Station Agent is more likely to make a mistake
    D. passenger has more difficulty picking up the change

14.______

15. The subway line which has a station NEAREST to Radio City Music Hall is the ______ Line.
    A. 6th Avenue
    B. Lexington Avenue
    C. Broadway—7th Avenue
    D. 8th Avenue

15.______

16. A passenger appears at your booth and makes loud and unreasonable complaints about the subway service.
    Your BEST action would be to
    A. show the passenger his error
    B. notify your superior
    C. call a transit patrolman
    D. listen without comment

16.______

Questions 17-24.

DIRECTIONS: Questions 17 through 24 in Column I are questions of simple arithmetic, each of which has one of the answers listed in Column II. Indicate the CORRECT answer for each question.

COLUMN I	COLUMN II	
17. 216 times 9	A. 1267	17.______
18. 46656 divided by 3 divided by 8	B. 2376	18.______
	C. 1944	
19. 2881 minus 468 minus 337	D. 1867	19.______
20. 198 times 3 times 4	E. 2184	20.______
21. 837 plus 18 plus 412	H. 2076	21.______
22. 8869 divided by 7		22.______
23. 2693 minus 509		23.______
24. 1489 plus 378		24.______

25. If you feel that your supervisor is unsympathetic towards you while you are being trained after your appointment as Station Agent, your BEST bet is to 25.______
    A. request a change in assignment to a location with a different supervisor
    B. insist on fairer treatment
    C. say nothing and try to learn as quickly as possible
    D. ask no questions even if in doubt

26. Station Agents are permitted to *pick* their tour of duty in order of their seniority. A Station Agent is NOT permitted to mutually exchange his selected tour with another station agent regardless of the circumstances. The MOST logical reason for this limitation is that otherwise 26.______
    A. the Station Agent next below in seniority will be unfairly treated
    B. tours might be bought and sold
    C. there would be too many changes in the assignment records
    D. newer employees might have a more important tour than the more experienced employees

27. Stuyvesant Town is located NEAREST to 27.______
    A. Peter Cooper Village
    B. Parkchester
    C. Bellevue Hospital
    D. Knickerbocker Village

28. A Station Agent gave the following change for a dollar bill: five dimes, five nickels, and one quarter. 28.______
As a general practice, this procedure would be
A. *bad* because he might run short of nickels
B. *bad* because he might run short of dimes
C. *good* because he would have to count less change at the end of his tour
D. *good* because the passenger would not need dimes the next trip

29. Of the following qualifications, the one LEAST important for a Station Agent to have in the daily performance of his duties is 29.______
A. thorough knowledge of the rules
B. geographical knowledge of the city
C. knowledge of train routes
D. ability to judge people

30. In a given station, if there are twice as many paid passengers on Thursday as on Saturday, and one-half as many on Sunday as on Saturday, it follows that the number on Sunday is _______ as many as on Thursday. 30.______
A. four times B. twice
C. one-half D. one-quarter

31. The subway line which has a station NEAREST to Coney Island is the _______ Line. 31.______
A. Lexington Avenue
B. Broadway—7th Avenue
C. 8th Avenue
D. Broadway

32. A Station Agent receives notice, via bulletin order, of changes in any city-owned bus route which acts as a feeder for the subway in order for him to 32.______
A. avoid improper use of transfers
B. receive information for his personal convenience
C. answer correctly questions from the public
D. directly inform each passenger requesting such transfer

33. The rules of the TA strictly prohibit any employee who is in an unfit condition because of indulgence in intoxicating liquor from reporting for or being on duty. Such use of intoxicating liquor while on duty is taken so seriously PRIMARILY because it 33.______
A. tends to affect judgment
B. annoys some passengers
C. results in overcautiousness
D. is immoral

34. If you do not clearly understand a written bulletin order recently issued to all Station Agents, your BEST procedure would be to 34.______
A. wait until the order is clarified since other Station Agents are probably having difficulty
B. call the general superintendent
C. use your best judgment
D. check with your immediate superior or another Station Agent

35. Manhattan College is located NEAREST to 35.______
A. Baker Field of Columbia University
B. New York University
C. Bronx Park
D. Van Cortlandt Park

36. Dial telephones have replaced manually operated telephones on the transit system. 36.______
An IMPORTANT reason for this change is that the dial system telephone
A. provides faster service
B. saves desk space
C. looks better
D. prevents getting wrong numbers

37. If a Station Agent notices a person in the station acting in a definitely suspicious manner, the Station Agent should 37.______
A. lock his booth and go to the person and question him
B. request the next passenger to obtain a policeman
C. call his headquarters and report the matter
D. ignore the matter and wait for developments

38. The subway line which has a station NEAREST to Port Authority Bus Terminal is the _______ Line. 38.______
A. Broadway
B. 6th Avenue
C. Broadway—7th Avenue
D. 8th Avenue

39. Employees of the transit system are entitled to semi-annual passes which are valid until June 30th and then replaced by similar new passes of new color, valid until December 31st. In each case, a seven-day grace period is allowed making the newly issued passes valid from June 24th and December 25th, respectively. 39.______
The PROBABLE purpose of this grace period is to
A. permit reasonable time for exchange of these passes
B. allow time for printing of the new passes
C. detect fraudulent passes
D. permit Station Agents to become used to the new color

40. In case of accident, employees who witnessed the accident are required to make individual written reports on prescribed forms as soon as possible. 40.______
The MOST probable reason for not allowing a single group report signed by all witnesses is because such a report
A. is less likely to give the complete picture
B. provides no alternate source of information if lost
C. may contain unnecessary information
D. would require too many witnesses in case of a court action

Questions 41-48.

DIRECTIONS: Questions 41 through 48 are based on the instructions regarding unusual occurrences given below. Read these instructions carefully before answering these questions.

INSTRUCTIONS REGARDING UNUSUAL OCCURRENCES

A prompt report of every unusual occurrence will be made by telephone to the Station Supervisor's office, whether or not a written report is used. The telephone report should include the time, place, and a concise statement of the circumstances and action taken, including the names and addresses of passengers and the names and badge numbers of all employees and police officers involved. Details will be confirmed in a written report when requested. No unusual occurrence is too trivial to report.

If the occurrence is of an emergency nature, or one which cannot be handled by the station personnel, the Transit Police will be notified first and the Station Supervisor's office immediately thereafter.

Train whistle signals for help (one long, one short, one long and one short blasts of the whistle) will be given immediate response by station section employees.

41. When reporting an unusual occurrence, a Station Agent need NOT say 41.______
A. *where* it happened
B. *what* was done about it
C. *when* it occurred
D. *why* it happened

42. A telephone report of an unusual occurrence should be made by a Station Agent 42.______
A. if no police are present
B. only if the occurrence is serious
C. in every case
D. according to his judgment

43. A Station Agent must submit a written report of an unusual occurrence 43.______
A. so that the supervisor's office need not take the telephone message in writing
B. if the telephone report would be too long
C. to prove that the incident occurred
D. if it is requested

44. A Station Agent on duty in a change booth seeing a boy break a light on the subway platform should 44.______
   A. try to catch the boy
   B. call the Transit Police
   C. report the act by telephone
   D. take no action personally

45. A Station Agent, being a station section employee, who hears a train whistle signal for help should 45.______
   A. immediately determine the reason
   B. immediately call an ambulance to meet the train
   C. wait for information from the train crew
   D. immediately call his superior

46. The meaning of the whistle signal from a train is determined entirely by the 46.______
   A. length of each blast
   B. total number of blasts
   C. order in which the different blasts are given
   D. combination of the length, number, and order of the blasts

47. A prompt telephone report is MOST clearly required from a Station Agent who observed 47.______
   A. an exasperated passenger violently try to shake a vending machine
   B. a passenger fall on a station stairway
   C. two passengers arguing about pushing
   D. that car doors on a train are slow in closing

48. A train crew wishing help from station section employees MUST 48.______
   A. use a whistle signal only
   B. blow the whistle for an appreciable time
   C. blow a specified whistle signal
   D. use a special whistle carried by the crew

49. The TA maintains a lost property office at 73 Rockwell Place, Brooklyn. The establishment of such an office 49.______
   A. tends to encourage carelessness in losing articles
   B. simplifies the return of lost articles turned in
   C. insures the return of all lost articles
   D. encourages the turning in of lost articles by the finders

50. It is the responsibility of a Station Agent to see that the revenue collected by him corresponds with the turnstile counter readings in his station. Therefore, whenever a turnstile maintainer arrives at a station to work on a defective turnstile, it is reasonable to expect that the Station Agent would 50.______
   A. supervise the work done by the maintainer
   B. read the turnstile counter before and after the work is done
   C. watch the operation of the turnstile counter after the repairs have been completed
   D. help the maintainer repair the turnstile

KEY (CORRECT ANSWERS)

1. B
2. D
3. C
4. C
5. B

6. A
7. D
8. D
9. A
10. A

11. C
12. C
13. D
14. B
15. A

16. D
17. C
18. C
19. H
20. B

21. A
22. A
23. E
24. D
25. C

26. B
27. A
28. A
29. D
30. D

31. D
32. C
33. A
34. D
35. D

36. A
37. C
38. D
39. A
40. A

41. D
42. C
43. D
44. C
45. A

46. D
47. B
48. C
49. B
50. B

TEST 5

DIRECTIONS: Each question or incomplete statement is followed by several suggested answers or completions. Select the one that BEST answers the question or completes the statement. *PRINT THE LETTER OF THE CORRECT ANSWER IN THE SPACE AT THE RIGHT.*

1. The Museum of Natural History is located NEAREST to 1.______
   A. Central Park Zoo B. Columbus Circle
   C. Metropolitan Museum of Art D. Hayden Planetarium

2. The TA instructions provide that all requests for ambulance service be made through the Transit Police Bureau. 2.______
   A LOGICAL reason for clearing through this Bureau is
   A. to handle the problem of duplication of calls
   B. so that the police may investigate the need
   C. that summoning an ambulance is a very complicated procedure
   D. because employees will be less likely to make unnecessary calls

3. A Station Agent must be constantly on the alert for counterfeit bills. 3.______
   A counterfeit bill is LEAST likely to differ from the genuine in the
   A. shade of ink used on the seal
   B. size of the bill
   C. letters preceding the serial number
   D. type of paper used

4. Employees are required to report promptly to superiors whenever they change their address PRIMARILY to 4.______
   A. permit contacting the employee in time of need
   B. assist the Post Office
   C. maintain discipline
   D. furnish correct information to outsiders upon request

5. Daily fare receipts are collected from the subway change booths by collection trains which operate at night. The collectors on these trains remove the money from the booth safes and return to the train. 5.______
   The MOST compelling reason for collecting at night is that
   A. fewer fares are received at night
   B. there are fewer passengers on the platform
   C. with less regular train service, less interference results
   D. it is safer from holdups

6. The subway line which has a station NEAREST to George Washington Bridge is the ________ Line. 6.______
   A. Broadway – 7th Ave.
   B. 8th Avenue
   C. Lexington Avenue
   D. 6th Avenue

7. A Station Agent is required to start his tour with a relatively small amount of change provided by the transit system. 7.______
The amount is small because
A. there will be less loss in case of a holdup
B. it is easier to account for a small amount
C. it keeps the Station Agent alert in making change
D. such change is money permanently tied up

8. To promote good public relations, it is MOST essential that a Station Agent learn how to 8.______
A. be tactful
B. judge character
C. handle large crowds
D. handle any emergencies well

Questions 9-12.

DIRECTIONS: Questions 9 through 12 are based on the instructions for packaging of bills as given below. Read these instructions carefully before answering these questions.

INSTRUCTIONS FOR PACKAGING OF BILLS
WHEN REMITTING CURRENCY

All bills must be faced in the same direction, with the portrait or face side up.

In remitting $1.00 bills, they should be forwarded in separate packages of $100.00 and $50.00 each, the balance to be tied in a separate package.

Bills of denomination larger than $1.00 and the remaining $1.00 bills (less than 50) should be arranged in a separate package with bills of the largest denomination on top. These are all tied together in one package which is called the odd package.

9. A Station Agent has $95, consisting of 55 $1.00 bills and 8 $5.00 bills, which he is packaging for remittance. He should place 9.______
A. the $1.00 bills with the portrait up and the $5.00 bills with the portrait down
B. the $5.00 bills with the portrait up and the $1.00 bills with the portrait down
C. all bills with the portrait down
D. all bills with the portrait up

10. A Station Agent has $200 in bills which is to be remitted. It consists of 5 $20.00 bills, 5 $10.00 bills, 5 $2.00 bills, and 40 $1.00 bills. 10.______
The number of packages that he should make is
A. 4 B. 3 C. 2 D. 1

11. A Station Agent has $187 all in $1.00 bills which is to be remitted. 11.______
The number of packages he should make it
A. 5 B. 4 C. 3 D. 2

12. A Station Agent has 5 packages each consisting of $1.00 bills only. 12.______
If the packaging was CORRECT, the total amount could be
A. $152 B. $294 C. $326 D. $368

13. The Port of New York Authority Bus Terminal is located NEAREST to 13.______
A. Battery Tunnel
B. Times Square
C. Radio City
D. Pennsylvania Station

14. A passenger complains to a Station Agent on duty in the change booth that the condition of a station toilet is very unsanitary. 14.______
The MOST reasonable action by the Station Agent would be to
A. immediately report the condition to his superior
B. notify the station porter
C. disregard the complaint
D. lock the change booth and inspect the toilet

15. Station Agents should be particularly alert when 15.______
A. making change
B. handling lost articles
C. receiving telephone orders
D. making up their reports

16. Station Agents should avoid unnecessary conversation with other employees MAINLY because it may 16.______
A. cause hard feelings by other employees
B. interfere with changemaking
C. cause suspicion
D. result in stolen change

17. Assume that the subway fare is now at two dollars and Metrocards are to be sold. 17.______
The city would lose the GREATEST amount of money if they were sold for
A. two for $3.90
B. three for $5.90
C. six for $11.90
D. seven for $13.90

18. Any objection that the riding public would have to the use of a well-designed Metrocard would MOST likely be that they 18.______
A. may be more easily lost than coins
B. would resent interference with their freedom
C. are not generally interchangeable with coins
D. would be confused with other cards

19. The turnstile counter readings at a certain station show that the greatest number of passengers enter this station between the hours of 7:00 A.M. and 9:00 A.M. on weekdays. 19.______
This is an indication that the station is MOST likely located in a
A. shopping center
B. residential area
C. manufacturing district
D. theatrical district

20. A Station Agent receives a general written order which he believes is unwise. The MOST appropriate action for the Station Agent to take would be to 20.______
A. disregard the order
B. request a change in the order
C. carry out the order
D. immediately consult several other Station Agents

21. Station Agents are cautioned not to tamper with the electric fans in the change booths in any way but are instructed to report difficulties when encountered so that qualified persons can make the necessary adjustments. 21.______
This means that
A. no Station Agent is able to fix an electric fan
B. Station Agents have no responsibility for the electric fans
C. it is not practical to permit Station Agents to repair fans
D. a report should be made if the booth is uncomfortably hot

22. Many of the subway employees are instructed in first aid. 22.______
The MOST likely reason for this procedure is to
A. aid physically handicapped passengers
B. decrease the number of accidents
C. provide temporary emergency aid
D. eliminate the need for calling doctors in accident cases

23. If two written orders issued generally to Station Agents disagree in some respect, a Station Agent should 23.______
A. use his best judgment
B. follow the original order
C. call up the superintendent
D. follow the one with the latest date

24. Booklets entitled SAFETY INSTRUCTIONS FOR TRANSPORTATION EMPLOYEES are distributed to all employees. 24.______
Evidently these booklets are
A. of no value except when employees are on duty
B. intended to be personally beneficial to each employee
C. strictly confidential
D. primarily of advantage to management

25. In changing a larger coin or bill, a Station Agent should generally include more than one dime in the change MAINLY because 25.______
A. the passenger may be paying more than one fare
B. passengers are likely to object to larger coins
C. dimes are lighter to carry
D. dimes are easier to give out than other coins

26. The subway line which has a station located NEAREST to Yankee Stadium is the ________ Line. 26.______
A. Broadway – 7th Ave.
B. Broadway
C. 8th Avenue
D. 6th Avenue

27. When a Station Agent receives instructions in writing, he should make sure that they are 27.______
A. brief B. detailed
C. understood D. observed by everyone

28. Station Agents have either day or night assignments. They select their assignments in the order of seniority. 28.______
The MOST probable reason for using this method is to
A. give every employee the assignment he desires
B. reward length of service
C. discourage carelessness
D. give new employees preference in selection

29. In the operation of the subway system, the Sunday schedule is GENERALLY used on a legal holiday because passenger traffic is 29.______
A. about the same on both days
B. heavier on weekdays than holidays
C. heaviest on Sundays and holidays
D. never heavy on a holiday

30. A person trips on a station stairway, striking his head so severely that his breathing is stopped. 30.______
First aid treatment should consist of the immediate application of
A. a bandage B. A compress
C. cold water D. artificial respiration

31. Ordinarily, dogs on a leash are not allowed to accompany passengers in subway cars because the dogs are 31.______
A. unsightly B. not used to trains
C. a nuisance D. not muzzled

32. When a passenger becomes seriously ill, it is advisable to call an ambulance PRIMARILY to 32.______
A. save expense for the city
B. provide adequate treatment
C. save money for the passenger
D. remove him from city property

33. The MOST convenient way of explaining the location of a certain gum vending machine to a repairman is by giving 33.______
A. its distance in feet from one end of the platform
B. the number of columns from one end of the platform to it
C. its distance in feet from the edge of the platform
D. the number of columns from it to the edge of the platform

34. An efficient Station Agent is one who 34.______
A. is well-educated
B. is always doing something
C. performs his duties well
D. has a congested station

35. The MAIN use for electricity in all subway change booths is for 35.______
A. air conditioning B. signaling
C. heating D. lighting

36. A Station Agent who has a deficit is one who has a 36.______
A. physical defect B. physical handicap
C. shortage in his accounts D. lack of personality

37. Employees are occasionally stationed at the exit gates of a subway station to 37.______
A. open the gates for passengers
B. prevent people from entering
C. watch for pickpockets
D. check on employees leaving the station

38. Station Agents are required to be bonded. 38.______
The MOST probable reason for this is
A. to encourage honesty
B. because they handle money
C. to discourage robbery
D. to provide funds for the government

39. Male Station Agents on duty are normally required to wear a collar and tie properly adjusted and generally present a neat and tidy appearance. 39.______
The MOST probable reason for this rule is to
A. prevent an unfavorable impression on passengers
B. make all Station Agents dress alike
C. train Station Agents to dress well
D. permit them to be readily identified a subway employees

40. Revenue is collected from change booths by collection parties. 40.______
The PRIMARY reason why each Station Agent does not bring his own receipts to a central office is that
A. each Station Agent would have more money than he could handle
B. such a procedure is not considered to be safe
C. each Station Agent is bonded
D. the collection party can not be robbed

41. Station Agents are provided with exact forms for all their work. 41.______
This is necessary PRINCIPALLY because
A. their work is very complicated
B. it keeps them occupied
C. the subway is owned by the city
D. there are hundreds of Station Agents doing the same work

42. Transfers on subway lines are USUALLY issued to 42.______
A. permit return trips for the same fare
B. reduce congestion
C. get people to use the subways
D. provide a greater variety of routes for one fare

43. Bronx-Whitestone Bridge connects the Bronx and 43.______
A. Queens B. Brooklyn C. Westchester D. Manhattan

44. The LEAST important thing to remember in answering the booth telephone is to 44.______
A. identify yourself
B. answer promptly even if busy
C. be abrupt at all times
D. speak directly into the mouthpiece

45. All employees are sometimes directed to initial one copy of a particular bulletin. This practice 45.______
A. saves time in the distribution of bulletins
B. furnishes positive evidence that the employee saw the bulletin
C. proves that the employee understood the bulletin
D. provides a personal bulletin for each employee

46. Washington Square Park is located in 46.______
A. Manhattan B. Queens C. the Bronx D. Brooklyn

47. A newly appointed Station Agent should study his book of rules at every opportunity in order to 47.______
A. keep occupied
B. know his job as soon as possible
C. be popular with his superior
D. be able to justify his errors

48. A Station Agent should count the booth money when relieving another Station Agent and beginning his tour of duty in order to 48.______
A. detect any counterfeits
B. check on the other Station Agent's honesty
C. minimize arguments and fix responsibility
D. save time

49. The PRINCIPAL advantage of having the subway employees under Civil Service is to 49.______
A. make it difficult to fire employees for cause
B. permit veterans' preference
C. make certain all employees are promoted
D. insure that appointments are by merit and fitness

50. JFK Airport is located NEAREST to 50.______
A. Fort Hamilton B. Prospect Park
C. LaGuardia Airport D. Floyd Bennett Field

KEY (CORRECT ANSWERS)

1. D	16. B	31. C	46. A
2. A	17. A	32. B	47. B
3. B	18. C	33. B	48. C
4. A	19. B	34. C	49. D
5. C	20. C	35. D	50. D
6. B	21. C	36. C	
7. D	22. C	37. B	
8. A	23. D	38. B	
9. D	24. B	39. A	
10. D	25. A	40. B	
11. C	26. D	41. D	
12. D	27. C	42. D	
13. B	28. B	43. A	
14. B	29. A	44. C	
15. C	30. D	45. B	

EXAMINATION SECTION

TEST 1

DIRECTIONS: Each question or incomplete statement is followed by several suggested answers or completions. Select the one that BEST answers the question of completes the statement. *PRINT THE LETTER OF THE CORRECT ANSWER IN THE SPACE AT THE RIGHT.*

Questions 1-13.

DIRECTIONS: The following is a Daily Fare Report, which is similar to one used by Station Agents for making a record of daily fares at a booth location. Questions 1 through 13, inclusive, are based SOLELY on this Report. Some of the required entries of the Report have been omitted, and a lettered entry, such as Entry F, has been inserted in their place. In answering a question related to a lettered entry, you are to compute the correct number that should appear in its place in the Report. To determine the correct number for a lettered entry, such as Entry F, it may be helpful to you to look at a similar completed portion of the Report to see how the entry in the similar completed portion was computed.

NOTE: The terms *Opening Reading* and *Closing Reading* in the Report refer to the amount of tokens as read on the turnstile meters in a station.

DAILY FARE REPORT

Division: BMT | Date: 3/23 | Booth No. 77

Clerk: John Doe Time: From 8 A.M. to 4 P.M.				Clerk: Mary Jane Time: From 4 P.M. to 12 Midnight		
		TURNSTILES				
Turn-stile No.	Opening Reading at 8 AM	Closing Reading at 4 PM	Differ-ence	Opening Reading at 4 PM	Closing Reading at 12 Midnight	Differ-ence
1	5246	5573	327	5573	5992	419
2	3918	4107	Entry F	4107	4575	468
3	2781	3127	346	3127	Entry G	298
4	6019	6252	233	Entry M	6398	146
Totals	17964	Entry I	1095	19059	20390	Entry J

Total Fares	1095	Total Fares	1331
Deduct: Slugs and Foreign Coins	6	Deduct: Slugs and Foreign Coins	3
Net Fares	1089	Net Fares	Entry K
(a) Net Fares at Value	Entry L	(a) Net Fares at Value	$2658.00

FARE RESERVE

Fare Reserve at Start Add: Fares Received	2250 1500	Fare Reserve at Start Add: Fares Received	2900 1000
Total Fare Reserve	Entry M	Total Fare Reserve	3900
Deduct: Total Reserve at End	2900	Deduct: Total Reserve at End	Entry N
Number of Reserve Fares Sold	850	Number of Reserve Fares Sold	725
(b) Value of Reserve Fares Sold	$1700.00	(b) Value of Reserve Fares Sold	Entry O
Net Amount Due: (a) +(b)	$3878.00	Net Amount Due: (a) +(b)	$4108.00

1. Entry F for Doe's tour of duty should be a DIFFERENCE OF 1.______
   A. 189 B. 199 C. 209 D. 299

2. Entry G for Jane's tour of duty should be a *closing reading* of 2.______
   A. 2829 B. 3315 C. 3325 D. 3425

3. Entry H for Jane's tour of duty should be an *opening reading* of 3.______
   A. 5252 B. 6152 C. 6252 D. 6552

4. Entry I for Doe's tour of duty should be a TOTAL of 4.______
   A. 18949 B. 19049 C. 19059 D. 19959

5. Entry J for Jane's tour of duty should be a TOTAL DIFFERENCE of 5.______
   A. 1221 B. 1231 C. 1321 D. 1331

6. Entry K for Jane's tour of duty should indicate that the NET FARES are 6.______
   A. 1328 B. 1334 C. 1338 D. 1344

7. Entry L for Doe's tour of duty should indicate that the NET FARES at token value amount to 7.______
   A. $1089.00 B. $1633.50 C. $2178.00 D. $2722.50

8. Entry M for Doe's tour of duty should indicate a TOTAL FARE RESERVE of 8.______
   A. 3700 B. 3750 C. 3850 D. 4250

9. Entry N for Jane's tour of duty should indicate that the TOTAL RESERVE at end should be 9.______
   A. 2175 B. 3175 C. 3185 D. 4625

10. Entry O for Jane's tour of duty should show that the value of RESERVE FARES SOLD should be 10.______
    A. $725.00 B. $1450.00 C. $1812.50 D. $2175.00

11. The number of passengers using Turnstile No. 3 from 8 A.M. to 12 Midnight is 11.______
A. 534 B. 544 C. 634 D. 644

12. The TOTAL NUMBER of reserve fares sold from 8 A.M. to 12 Midnight is 12.______
A. 850 B. 1575 C. 2900 D. 3175

13. The TOTAL number of passengers using Turnstile Nos. 1 and 4 from 8 A.M. to 4 P.M. is 13.______
A. 550 B. 560 C. 746 D. 1125

Questions 14-19.

DIRECTIONS: Questions 14 through 19, inclusive, are to be answered on the basis of the paragraphs below, which represent sample instructions given to Station Agents regarding the handling of money. Read the paragraphs carefully before answering the questions. In answering the questions, consider ONLY the information included in the paragraphs.

If a passenger presents currency or coin of doubtful or questionable validity or mutilated currency of coins to a Station Agent, the money should be courteously refused and returned.

Upon detecting an actual counterfeit, the Station Agent must confiscate it and give a receipt to the party who presented it. The receipt should be prepared in duplicate and must contain the name and address of the person who presented the counterfeit, and a description of the counterfeit, including denomination, date, numbers, and series. The party who presented the counterfeit should be advised that any further information regarding the counterfeit must be obtained from the Revenue Department at 370 Jay Street, Brooklyn. The counterfeit and the carbon copy of the receipt should be placed immediately in the prescribed envelope for remittance with the current day's receipts.

Under no circumstances will a Station Agent allow a counterfeit to pass from his possession, except by remittance to the Revenue Department, or by special authority of the Superintendent, Stations.

Station Agents should not attempt to arrest a person who presents a counterfeit. However, in the event that the person becomes disorderly, the Transit Police should be requested to handle the situation.

14. If a passenger presents a Station Agent with a $5 bill of doubtful validity, the Station Agent should 14.______
A. call a Transit Policeman
B. confiscate the $5 bill
C. return the $5 bill
D. accept the $5 bill

15. When a Station Agent confiscates a counterfeit $5 bill from a passenger, the Station Agent should 15.______
A. hold the passenger for the Transit Police
B. destroy the $5 bill
C. inform the Treasury Department
D. give the passenger a receipt

16. Any confiscated counterfeit dollar bills should be put in the prescribed envelope 16.______
    A. and mailed to the U.S. Treasury Department
    B. along with that day's receipts
    C. and destroyed
    D. along with the current weekly receipts

17. A Station Agent may allow a counterfeit to pass from his possession 17.______
    A. if he has obtained a receipt for it
    B. by remitting it to the Revenue Department
    C. by special authority of his Station Supervisor
    D. by remitting it to the Transit Police

18. A passenger has presented a Station Agent with a counterfeit $5 bill. 18.______
    The Station Agent should
    A. attempt to arrest the passenger
    B. not attempt to arrest the passenger
    C. immediately call the Transit Police
    D. immediately notify the Superintendent, Stations

19. If a person who presents counterfeit money to a Station Agent wants additional information, he should be told to contact the 19.______
    A. Transit Police
    B. Superintendent, Stations
    C. Revenue Department
    D. Metropolitan Transit Authority

20. The PRIMARY reason for requiring new employees to attend training classes is that 20.______
    A. it gives employees the opportunity to learn about other jobs
    B. it gives employees a chance to meet the supervisors
    C. most new employees have not previously held a regular full-time job
    D. most new employees do not know the specific department procedures in a new job

21. If you were to arrange the names Marcy, Marcon, Marcel, and Marchess in alphabetical order, the THIRD name should be 21.______
    A. Marcel B. Marcy C. Marchess D. Marcon

22. If you were to arrange the names Starton, Starttin, Starmon, and Starret in alphabetical order, the order would be: 22.______
    A. Starmon, Starret, Starttin, Starton
    B. Starmon, Starret, Starton, Starttin
    C. Starret, Starmon, Starton, Starttin
    D. Starret, Starton, Starmon, Starttin

23. Many employees are given first-aid instructions in order to 23.______
    A. eliminate accidents on the job
    B. eliminate the need for calling a doctor
    C. prepare them for promotion
    D. prepare them to give emergency aid

24. All employees receive a book of rules and regulations. If an employee does not understand any rule, he should 24.______
    A. disregard it
    B. interpret it as best he can
    C. request an explanation from his supervisor
    D. protest the rule

25. Employees are required to submit a report immediately of any occurrence when they use supplies from one of the first-aid kits. 25.______
    The MOST logical reason for this rule is that
    A. the employee can gain credit for his actions
    B. the first-aid kit can be marked *USED*
    C. it facilitates the replacement of used supplies
    D. the first-aid kit can be properly sealed

26. While working, an employee is MOST apt to avoid accidental injury if he 26.______
    A. keeps mentally alert
    B. works by himself
    C. works very rapidly
    D. knows first aid

27. In general, the GREATEST value of writing out an accident report after an accident is to provide 27.______
    A. a record of each accident
    B. evidence for use in a court case
    C. a method for properly placing blame on the person responsible for the accident
    D. information that may be useful in preventing other accidents

28. It is important to be courteous to passengers PRIMARILY to 28.______
    A. maintain good relations with the public
    B. provide cleaner stations
    C. keep the transit system safer
    D. reduce vandalism

29. If you do not understand a verbal order that your supervisor gives you, it would be BEST if you were to 29.______
    A. ask another employee to explain the order
    B. ask your supervisor to explain the order
    C. carry out the order to the best of your ability
    D. do nothing until your supervisor asks you about it

30. As a newly appointed employee, you will be expected by your supervisor to 30.______
    A. perform your work perfectly, right from the start
    B. know the job routines with no training
    C. pay close attention to instructions
    D. perform very little work for the first few months

KEY (CORRECT ANSWERS)

1. A	11. D	21. D
2. D	12. B	22. B
3. C	13. B	23. D
4. C	14. C	24. C
5. D	15. D	25. C
6. A	16. B	26. A
7. C	17. B	27. D
8. B	18. B	28. A
9. B	19. C	29. B
10. B	20. D	30. C

EXAMINATION SECTION

TEST 1

DIRECTIONS: Each question or incomplete statement is followed by several suggested answers or completions. Select the one that BEST answers the question of completes the statement. *PRINT THE LETTER OF THE CORRECT ANSWER IN THE SPACE AT THE RIGHT.*

Questions 1-16.

DIRECTIONS: Questions 1 through 16 are to be answered on the basis of the Daily Fare Report shown below. When answering these questions, refer to this Report. Some of the required entries of the Report have been omitted on purpose, and a lettered entry, such as ENTRY F, is shown in place of the proper number that should appear in that space. In answering the questions concerning the lettered entries, you are to compute the correct number that should be in the space where the lettered entry is located.

DAILY FARE REPORT

Division: IND | Date: 3/12 | Booth No. S-50

Name: John Brown Time: From 7 A.M. to 3 P.M.	Name: Mary Smith Time: From 3 P.M. to 11 P.M.

TURNSTILES

Turn-stile	Opening Reading	Closing Reading	Differ-ence	Opening Reading	Closing Reading	Differ-ence
1	5123	5410	287	5410	6019	609
2	3442	ENTRY F	839	4281	4683	402
3	8951	9404	453	ENTRY G	9757	353
4	7663	8265	602	8265	8588	ENTRY H
Totals	ENTRY I	27360	2181	27360	ENTRY J	1687

Total Fares	2181	Total Fares	1687
Deduct: Slugs and Foreign Coins	12	Deduct: Slugs and Foreign Coins	ENTRY K
Deduct: Test Rings-Turnstile	0	Deduct: Test Rings Turnstile #3	3
Net Fares	2169		
(a) Net Fares at Fare Value	ENTRY L	(a) Net Fares at Fare Value	$1680.00
Fare Reserve at Start	4200	Fare Reserve at Start	5000
Add: Fares Received	2200	Add: Fares Received	ENTRY M
Deduct: Fares transferred out	1400	Deduct: Fares transferred out	0
Total Fare Reserve	ENTRY N	Total Fare Reserve	6450
Deduct: Total Reserve at End	4300	Deduct: Total Reserve at End	5674
No. of Reserve Fares Sold	670	No. of Reserve Fares Sold	ENTRY O
(b) Value of Reserve Fares Sold	ENTRY P	(b) Value of Reserve Fares Sold	$776.00
Net Amount Due: (a)+(b)	$2839.00	Net Amount Due: (a)+(b)	ENTRY Q

1. ENTRY F for Brown's tour of duty should be a closing reading of 1.______
A. 2603 B. 3873 C. 4281 D. 4671

2. ENTRY G for Smith's tour of duty should be an opening reading of 2.______
A. 8642 B. 3932 C. 9404 D. 9857

3. ENTRY H for Smith's tour of duty should be a difference of 3.______
A. 303 B. 323 C. 344 D. 402

4. ENTRY I for Brown's tour of duty should be a total of 4.______
A. 24299 B. 25179 C. 26288 D. 27168

5. ENTRY J for Smith's tour of duty should be a total of 5.______
A. 28036 B. 29047 C. 29556 D. 30437

6. ENTRY K for Smith's tour of duty should indicate that the number of slugs and foreign coins is 6.______
A. 0 B. 2 C. 4 D. 7

7. ENTRY L for Brown's tour of duty should indicate that the net fares amount to 7.______
A. $1411.00 B. $1549.00 C. $1859.00 D. $2169.00

8. ENTRY M for Smith's tour of duty should indicate that the fares received number 8.______
A. 674 B. 1000 C. 1200 D. 1450

9. ENTRY N for Brown's tour of duty should indicate a total fare reserve of 9.______
A. 670 B. 5000 C. 6400 D. 7800

10. ENTRY O for Smith's tour of duty should indicate that the number of reserve fares sold was 10.______
A. 776 B. 1450 C. 3250 D. 12124

11. ENTRY P for Brown's tour of duty should indicate that the value of reserve fares sold should be 11.______
A. $600.00 B. $670.00 C. $1400.00 D. $1495.00

12. ENTRY Q for Smith's tour of duty should indicate that the net amount due is 12.______
A. $2456.00 B. $1367.00 C. $906.00 D. $774.00

13. The number of passengers using Turnstile No. 2 from 7 A.M. to 11 P.M. is 13.______
A. 1241 B. 839 C. 402 D. 287

14. The turnstile showing the GREATEST use from 7 A.M. to 3 P.M. is No. 14.______
A. 1 B. 2 C. 3 D. 4

15. The TOTAL fares for all turnstiles from 7 A.M. to 11 P.M. amounted to 15.______
A. 1687 B. 2181 C. 3868 D. 4275

16. The TOTAL net fares from 7 A.M. to 11 P.M. amounted to 16.______
A. 1680 B. 2169 C. 3849 D. 3868

Questions 17-21.

DIRECTIONS: Questions 17 through 21 are to be answered on the basis of the chart of Hourly Turnstile Readings shown below. Refer to this chart when answering these questions.

HOURLY TURNSTILE READINGS

TURNSTILE NO.	7:00 A.M.	8:00 A.M.	9:00 A.M.	10:00 A.M.	11:00 A.M.
1	37111	37905	38342	38451	38485
2	78432	79013	79152	79237	79306
3	45555	45921	45989	46143	46233
4	89954	90063	90121	90242	90299

17. The total number of passengers using Turnstile No. 1 from 7:00 A.M. to 11:00 A.M. is 17.______
A. 580 B. 794 C. 1374 D. 1594

18. The turnstile which registered the LARGEST number of fares from 7:00 A.M. to 8:00 A.M. is No. 18.______
A. 1 B. 2 C. 3 D. 4

19. The total number of passengers using all four turnstiles between 10:00 A.M. and 11:00 A.M. is 19.______
A. 57 B. 250 C. 396 D. 3271

20. Turnstile No. 4 registered the HIGHEST number of passengers between ________ A.M. and ________ A.M. 20.______
A. 7:00; 8:00 B. 8:00; 9:00
C. 9:00; 10:00 D. 10:00; 11:00

21. The turnstile which registered the LOWEST number of passengers between 8:00 A.M. and 9:00 A.M. is No. 21.______
A. 1 B. 2 C. 3 D. 4

22. If a passenger wants to obtain 3 fares without getting any change, he should give a Station Agent 22.______
A. 26 quarters, 8 dimes, and 4 nickels
B. 24 quarters, 8 dimes, and 4 nickels
C. 26 quarters
D. 60 dimes and 10 nickels

23. If a passenger wants to obtain 25 fares and to get no cents in change, he should give a Station Agent the following amount: 23.______
A. $50.00 B. $60.50 C. $62.50 D. $80.00

Questions 24-31.

DIRECTIONS: Questions 24 through 31 involve various places of interest in New York City. Column I lists the places of interest, while Column II lists four of the boroughs of New York City. For the question number involved, indicate the letter preceding the borough where the place of interest is located.

	COLUMN I	COLUMN II	
24.	New York Aquarium	A. Bronx	24.______
25.	Carnegie Hall	B. Brooklyn	25.______
26.	Citi Field	C. Manhattan	26.______
27.	Lincoln Center	D. Queens	27.______
28.	Sheepshead Bay		28.______
29.	Van Cortlandt Park		29.______
30.	La Guardia Airport		30.______
31.	New York Coliseum		31.______

32. The train whistle or horn signal that means the train crew needs assistance consists of 32.______
    A. one long, one short, one long, one short blast
    B. two long, two short blasts
    C. a succession of short sounds
    D. four short blasts

33. Emergency alarm boxes are used to remove power from the third rail. The location of these alarm boxes along the roadway is indicated by ________ light(s). 33.______
    A. a blue B. a yellow
    C. a red D. 3 amber

34. According to the rules and regulations, soda acid fire extinguishers should NOT be used on fires 34.______
    A. involving wood or paper
    B. in well ventilated areas
    C. involving stored combustible material
    D. of an electrical nature

35. An employee is NOT permitted to give a passenger the description of any lost article which the employee has found and turned in PRIMARILY because 35.______
A. the employee may make a mistake in the description
B. this would delay the employee in his work
C. this might aid the passenger in claiming property not belonging to him
D. employees are not permitted to hold conversations with passengers

36. There is NOT direct subway route between 36.______
A. Queens and Brooklyn B. Manhattan and Bronx
C. Manhattan and Brooklyn D. Bronx and Queens

37. A Station Agent is permitted to take temporary charge of a turnstile maintainer's tools 37.______
A. under no circumstances
B. provided he notifies his station supervisor first
C. for a period of time not over 1 hour
D. for a period of time not over 3 hours

38. Bagging time is the interval of time when 38.______
A. a Station Agent collects fares from the turnstiles
B. a Station Agent closes out his fare report and prepares his receipts for remittance
C. revenue bags are collected by collecting agents
D. coins are counted by the coin counting machine and deposited in bags

39. Safety rules are MOST useful because they 39.______
A. fix responsibility for accidents
B. prevent negligence
C. make it less necessary to think
D. indicate ways of avoiding hazards

40. For the purpose of supervision and administration, the stations of the Transit Authority are divided into ________ territorial zones. 40.______
A. 4 B. 6 C. 8 D. 10

KEY (CORRECT ANSWERS)

1. C	11. B	21. D	31. C
2. C	12. A	22. A	32. A
3. B	13. A	23. C	33. A
4. B	14. B	24. B	34. D
5. B	15. C	25. C	35. C
6. C	16. C	26. D	36. D
7. D	17. C	27. C	37. A
8. D	18. A	28. B	38. B
9. B	19. B	29. A	39. D
10. A	20. C	30. D	40. C

TEST 2

DIRECTIONS: Each question or incomplete statement is followed by several suggested answers or completions. Select the one that BEST answers the question of completes the statement. *PRINT THE LETTER OF THE CORRECT ANSWER IN THE SPACE AT THE RIGHT.*

NOTE: The worth of a token shall be considered to be $2.75.

1. A passenger gives a Station Agent $17.80 and requests 6 fares. The Station Agent should give the passenger 6 fares and ________ in change. 1.______
   A. $1.20 B. $1.30 C. $1.40 D. $2.00

2. The MAXIMUM number of fares a passenger should get when he gives a Station Agent $10.00 is 2.______
   A. 5 B. 4 C. 3 D. 2

3. If a passenger wants to obtain 15 fares without getting any change, he should give a Station Agent EXACTLY 3.______
   A. $34.00 B. $39.25 C. $41.25 D. $42.00

4. A passenger who purchased 7 fares and received $1 in change from a Station Agent MOST likely gave the Station Agent a total of 4.______
   A. $19.10 B. $19.25 C. $20.00 D. $20.25

5. The total amount of money represented by 43 half-dollars, 26 quarters, and 71 dimes is 5.______
   A. $28.00 B. $35.10 C. $44.30 D. $56.60

6. The total amount of money represented by 132 quarters, 97 dimes, and 220 nickels is 6.______
   A. $43.70 B. $44.20 C. $52.90 D. $53.70

7. The total amount of money represented by 40 quarters, 40 dimes, and 20 nickels is 7.______
   A. $14.50 B. $15.00 C. $15.50 D. $16.00

8. The sum of $29.61 + $101.53 + $943.64 is 8.______
   A. $983.88 B. $1074.78 C. $1174.98 D. $1341.42

9. The sum of $132.25 + $85.63 + $7056.44 is 9.______
   A. $1694.19 B. $7274.32 C. $8464.57 D. $9346.22

10. The sum of 4010 + 1271 + 838 + 23 is 10.______
    A. 6142 B. 6162 C. 6242 D. 6362

11. The sum of 53632 + 27403 + 98765 + 75424 is 11.______
    A. 19214 B. 215214 C. 235224 D. 255224

12. The sum of 76342 + 49050 + 21206 + 59989 is 12.______
    A. 196586 B. 206087 C. 206587 D. 234487

13. The sum of $452.13 + $963.45 + $621.25 is 13.______
A. $1936.83 B. $2036.83 C. $2095.73 D. $2135.73

14. The sum of 36392 + 42156 + 98765 is 14.______
A. 167214 B. 177203 C. 177313 D. 178213

15. The sum of 40125 + 87123 + 24689 is 15.______
A. 141827 B. 151827 C. 151937 D. 161947

16. The sum of 2379 + 4015 + 6521 + 9986 is 16.______
A. 22901 B. 22819 C. 21801 D. 21791

17. From 50962 subtract 36197. 17.______
The answer should be
A. 14675 B. 14765 C. 14865 D. 24765

18. From 9000 subtract 31928. 18.______
The answer should be
A. 58072 B. 59062 C. 68172 D. 69182

19. From 63764 subtract 21548. 19.______
The answer should be
A. 42216 B. 43122 C. 45126 D. 85312

20. From $9605.13 subtract $2715.96. 20.______
The answer should be
A. $12,321.09 B. $8.690.16
C. $6,990.07 D. $6,889.17

21. From 76421 subtract 73101. 21.______
The answer should be
A. 3642 B. 3540 C. 3320 D. 3242

22. From $8.25 subtract $6.50. 22.______
The answer should be
A. $1.25 B. $1.50 C. $1.75 D. $2.25

23. Multiply 563 by 0.50. 23.______
The answer should be
A. 281.50 B. 28.15 C. 2.815 D. 0.2815

24. Multiply 0.35 by 1045. 24.______
The answer should be
A. 0.36575 B. 3.6575 C. 36.575 D. 365.75

25. Multiply 25 by 2513. 25.______
The answer should be
A. 62825 B. 62725 C. 60825 D. 52825

26. Multiply 423 by 0.01.
The answer should be
A. 0.0423 B. 0.423 C. 4.23 D. 42.3
26.______

27. Multiply 6.70 by 3.2.
The answer should be
A. 2.1440 B. 21.440 C. 214.40 D. 2144.0
27.______

28. Multiply 630 by 517.
The answer should be
A. 325,710 B. 345,720 C. 362,425 D. 385,660
28.______

29. Multiply 35 by 846.
The answer should be
A. 4050 B. 9450 C. 18740 D. 29610
29.______

30. Multiply 823 by 0.05.
The answer should be
A. 0.4115 B. 4.115 C. 41.15 D. 411.50
30.______

31. Multiply 1690 by 0.10.
The answer should be
A. 0.169 B. 1.69 C. 16.90 D. 169.0
31.______

32. Divide 2765 by 35.
The answer should be
A. 71 B. 79 C. 87 D. 93
32.______

33. From $18.55 subtract $6.80.
The answer should be
A. $9.75 B. $10.95 C. $11.75 D. $25.35
33.______

34. The sum of 2.75 + 4.50 + 3.60 is
A. 9.75 B. 10.85 C. 11.15 D. 11.95
34.______

35. The sum of 9.63 + 11.21 + 17.25 is
A. 36.09 B. 38.09 C. 39.92 D. 41.22
35.______

36. The sum of 112.0 + 16.9 + 3.84 is
A. 129.3 B. 132.74 C. 136.48 D. 167.3
36.______

37. When 65 is added to the result of 14 multiplied by 13, the answer is
A. 92 B. 182 C. 247 D. 16055
37.______

38. From $391.55 subtract $273.45.
The answer should be
A. $118.10 B. $128.20 C. $178.10 D. $218.20
38.______

39. When 119 is subtracted from the sum of 2016 + 1634, the answer is 39.______
A. 2460 B. 3531 C. 3650 D. 3769

40. Multiply 35 x 65 x 15. 40.______
The answer should be
A. 2275 B. 24265 C. 31145 D. 34125

KEY (CORRECT ANSWERS)

1. B	11. D	21. C	31. D
2. C	12. C	22. C	32. B
3. C	13. B	23. A	33. C
4. D	14. C	24. D	34. B
5. B	15. C	25. A	35. B
6. D	16. A	26. C	36. B
7. B	17. B	27. B	37. C
8. B	18. A	28. A	38. A
9. B	19. A	29. D	39. B
10. A	20. D	30. C	40. D

EXAMINATION SECTION
TEST 1

DIRECTIONS: Each question or incomplete statement is followed by several suggested answers or completions. Select the one that BEST answers the question of completes the statement. *PRINT THE LETTER OF THE CORRECT ANSWER IN THE SPACE AT THE RIGHT.*

Questions 1-13.

DIRECTIONS: Questions 1 through 13 are to be answered on the basis of the MONEY CHART below. Each line contains a date and a listing of the number of coins of each denomination received on that date.

MONEY CHART

Date	Nickels	Dimes	Quarters	Half Dollars
August 1	134	284	103	1
August 2	241	129	79	3
August 3	313	357	156	2
August 4	437	291	207	4
August 5	962	835	81	3
August 6	442	276	132	1
August 7	589	437	216	0
August 8	812	799	344	4
August 9	651	701	116	2
August 10	713	829	95	3

1. What was the value of the quarters received on August 1? 1.____

   A. $24.75 B. $25.25 C. $25.50 D. $25.75

2. What was the value of the quarters received on August 4? 2.____

   A. $50.75 B. $51.25 C. $51.75 D. $52.25

3. What was the value of the quarters received on August 8 and August 9? 3.____

   A. $115.00 B. $116.00 C. $117.00 D. $118.00

4. What was the value of the dimes received during the period of August 5 through August 8? 4.____

   A. $214.60 B. $222.60 C. $233.70 D. $234.70

5. What was the value of the nickels received on August 2 and August 3? 5.____

   A. $25.60 B. $26.75 C. $27.70 D. $28.25

6. What was the value of the nickels received on August 5 and August 7? 6.____

   A. $76.85 B. $77.55 C. $77.75 D. $78.15

7. What was the value of the nickels and quarters received on August 6? 7.____

A. $54.50 B. $54.70 C. $54.90 D. $55.10

8. What was the value of the quarters received on August 7? 8.____

A. $53.75 B. $54.00 C. $54.25 D. $54.50

9. What was the value of the nickels received on August 4 and August 9? 9.____

A. $53.90 B. $54.10 C. $54.25 D. $54.40

10. What was the value of the quarters received on August 10? 10.____

A. $22.75 B. $23.25 C. $23.75 D. $24.25

11. What was the value of the nickels and quarters received on August 1 ? 11.____

A. $32.45 B. $32.55 C. $32.75 D. $32.85

12. What was the value of the dimes received on all of the days shown in the chart? 12.____

A. $246.90 B. $493.80 C. $1,234.50 D. $4,938.00

13. What was the value of all the coins received on August 4? 13.____

A. $102.70 B. $102.95 C. $104.70 D. $106.00

14. On which street in Manhattan is Macy's Department Store located? 14.____
_______ Street.

A. 14th B. 34th C. 42nd D. 59th

15. Which of the following bridges is CLOSEST to City Hall? 15.____
The______ Bridge.

A. Brooklyn
B. Williamsburg
C. 59th Street
D. George Washington

16. At which of the following is the New York Aquarium located? 16.____

A. Coney Island
B. South Ferry
C. Lincoln Center
D. Central Park

17. If a Station Agent earns $9.18 per hour and works a 40-hour week, his weekly pay will be 17.____

A. $357.20 B. $366.20 C. $366.40 D. $367.20

18. If a Station Agent earns $13.12 per hour and works a 40-hour week, how much will she receive in two weeks? 18.____

A. $1,049.60
B. $1,049.80
C. $1,050.60
D. $1,051.60

19. What is the value of 3 twenty-dollar bills, 5 ten-dollar bills, 13 five-dollar bills, and 43 one-dollar bills? 19.____

A. $218.00 B. $219.00 C. $220.00 D. $221.00

20. What is the value of 8 twenty-dollar bills, 13 ten-dollar bills, 27 five-dollar bills, 3 two-dollar bills, and 43 one-dollar bills? 20.____

A. $364.00 B. $374.00 C. $474.00 D. $485.00

21. What is the value of 6 twenty-dollar bills, 8 ten-dollar bills, 19 five-dollar bills, and 37 one-dollar bills? 21.____

A. $232.00 B. $233.00 C. $332.00 D. $333.00

22. What is the value of 13 twenty-dollar bills, 17 ten-dollar bills, 24 five-dollar bills, 7 two-dollar bills, and 55 one-dollar bills? 22.____

A. $594.00 B. $599.00 C. $609.00 D. $619.00

23. What is the value of 7 half dollars, 9 quarters, 23 dimes, and 17 nickels? 23.____

A. $7.80 B. $7.90 C. $8.80 D. $8.90

24. What is the value of 3 one-dollar coins, 3 half dollars, 7 quarters, 13 dimes, and 27 nickels? 24.____

A. $7.80 B. $8.70 C. $8.80 D. $8.90

Questions 25-27.

DIRECTIONS: Questions 25 through 27 are to be answered on the basis of the information contained in the FARE REPORT below. A Station Agent records the reading of the counter of each turnstile when he comes on duty, and does the same again one hour before he goes off duty. (The readings of the counters he records when he comes on duty are obtained from the Station Agent who is going off duty.)

FARE REPORT

Beginning At 0700 Hours ____ Mo. ______ Day ______ 20 ______
Tour Ending At 1500 Hours ____ Mo. ______ Day ______ 20 ______
Division ____________ Station ______________________

Turnstile	Opening Reading At 0600		Closing Reading At 1400		Difference	
1	06	343	07	214		871
2			54	472	1	615
3	91	703	92	365		
4	17	925	20	107	2	182
5						
6						-
7						
8						
9						
10						330
TOTAL	168	828			5	
ADD	Hand collections/Unregistered fares (explain in remarks)					
	TOTAL FARES					

25. What was the opening reading of Turnstile No. 2? 25.____

A. 52,766 B. 52,857 C. 52,868 D. 53,857

26. What was the difference between the opening reading and the closing reading of Turnstile No. 3? 26.____

A. 562 B. 568 C. 662 D. 668

27. What was the TOTAL of the closing readings of all four turnstiles? 27.____

A. 163,498 B. 173,158 C. 173,498 D. 174,158

Questions 28-35.

DIRECTIONS: Questions 28 through 35 are to be answered SOLELY on the basis of the REPORT OF HOURLY TURNSTILE READINGS below. The changes in the readings for each turnstile from hour to hour give the number of passengers who passed through that turnstile for each hour.

REPORT OF HOURLY TURNSTILE READINGS

TURN-STILE NO.	READ AT 1 AM	READ AT 2AM	READ AT 3AM	READ AT 4AM	READ AT 5AM	READ AT 6AM	READ AT 7AM	READ AT 8AM	DIFFERENCE FOR ENTIRE PERIOD
1	12319	12320	12326	12359	12367	12612	12913	13128	809
2	9121	9131	9217	9389	10146	10352	10465	10529	1408
3	13475	13484	13604	13718	13869		14207	14496	1021
4	14097	14099	14104	14112	14143	14287	14397	14601	
TOTAL	49012	49034	49251	49578		51170	51982	52754	3742

28. How many passengers entered through Turnstile No. 2 between 3 A.M. and 7 A.M.? 28.____

A. 1,247 B. 1,248 C. 1,257 D. 1,258

29. What was the TOTAL of the readings of the four turnstiles at 5 A.M.? 29.____

A. 50,404 B. 50,506 C. 50,525 D. 50,637

30. How many passengers entered through Turnstile No. 1 and No. 3 between 2 A.M. and 4 A.M.? 30.____

A. 273 B. 282 C. 291 D. 297

31. What was the reading of Turnstile No. 3 at 6 A.M.? 31.____

A. 13,875 B. 13,887 C. 13,902 D. 13,919

32. What was the difference in readings for the entire period for Turnstile No. 4? 32.____

A. 504 B. 513 C. 605 D. 614

33. How many passengers entered through the four turnstiles between 6 A.M. and 8 A.M.? 33.____

A. 1,574 B. 1,584 C. 1,674 D. 1,684

34. How many passengers entered through Turnstile No. 1 between 1 A.M. and 7A.M.? 34.____

A. 594 B. 597 C. 603 D. 604

35. How many passengers entered through Turnstile No. 2 and No. 4 between 5 A.M. and 8 A.M.? 35.____

A. 796 B. 822 C. 841 D. 851

36. A Station Agent has a quantity of consecutively numbered block transfers. The number on the block transfer having the lowest number is 27,069. The number on the block transfer having the highest number is 27,154. 36.____
How many block transfers does the Station Agent have?

A. 84 B. 85 C. 86 D. 87

37. A delay in train service on a subway line began at 5:53 A.M. and ended at 6:42 A.M. 37.____
How long was the delay?

A. 49 minutes B. 1 hour, 9 minutes
C. 1 hour, 11 minutes D. 1 hour, 29 minutes

38. A delay in train service on a subway line began at 11:48 A.M. and ended at 3:19 P.M. 38.____
How long was the delay?
_______ hours,_______ minutes.

A. 2; 31 B. 2; 57 C. 3; 31 D. 3; 57

39. A delay in train service on a subway line began at 1:57 P.M. and ended at 2:39 P.M. 39.____
How long was the delay?
_______ minutes.

A. 42 B. 52 C. 62 D. 82

40. If you have 7,438 fare cards and sell 3,989 of them, how many do you have left? 40.____

A. 3,449 B. 4,338 C. 4,551 D. 4,568

KEY (CORRECT ANSWERS)

1. D	11. A	21. C	31. D
2. C	12. B	22. D	32. A
3. A	13. C	23. D	33. B
4. D	14. B	24. D	34. A
5. C	15. A	25. B	35. C
6. B	16. A	26. C	36. C
7. D	17. D	27. D	37. A
8. B	18. A	28. B	38. C
9. D	19. A	29. C	39. A
10. C	20. C	30. A	40. A

TEST 2

DIRECTIONS: Each question or incomplete statement is followed by several suggested answers or completions. Select the one that BEST answers the question of completes the statement. *PRINT THE LETTER OF THE CORRECT ANSWER IN THE SPACE AT THE RIGHT.*

Questions 1 -5.

DIRECTIONS: Questions 1 through 5 are to be answered SOLELY on the basis of the information contained in the REMITTANCE REPORT below.

REMITTANCE REPORT

REMITTANCE			MONEY ROOM SUPERVISOR'S INITIALS	AMOUNT		MONEY ROOM CORRECTIONS	
BILLS	No. of Bills	Money Rm. Corrections		DOLLARS	CENTS		
Hundreds							
Fifties							
Twenties	37			740	00		
Tens	53			530	00		
Fives	79			395	00		
Twos	1			2	00		
Ones	539			539	00		
SUB-TOTAL BILLS							
COINS							
Dollars							
Halves				5	50		
Quarters				189	00		
Dimes				33	00		
Nickels				27	00		
Pennies				5	50		
NYCTA PAY CHECK NO. ______							
MISCELLANEOUS CHECK NO.							
TOTAL CASH REMITTANCE							

1. What was the value of all the bills remitted? 1.____

   A. $2,095 B. $2,116 C. $2,186 D. $2,206

2. What was the value of all the coins remitted? 2.____

   A. $239 B. $250 C. $260 D. $262

3. What was the value of the TOTAL remittance? 3.____

   A. $2,451 B. $2,466 C. $2,473 D. $2,481

4. How many quarters were remitted? 4.____

A. 189 B. 254 C. 570 D. 756

5. How many nickels were remitted? 5.____

A. 216 B. 260 C. 540 D. 740

6. Which of the following combinations of coins is the exact amount of money needed to buy four fares at $2.50 each? 6.____

______ half dollars, ______ quarters, ______ dimes, and ______ nickels.

A. 2; 14; 10; 8
B. 8; 6; 16; 16
C. 10; 10; 12; 26
D. 4; 16; 20; 38

7. A Station Agent begins her tour of duty with 2,322 fares. How many fares will she have at the end of her tour of duty if she sells 1,315 and collects 1,704 from the turnstiles during her tour of duty? 7.____

A. 2,687 B. 2,693 C. 2,711 D. 2,722

8. A Station Agent has three bags of fares. One contains 273 fares, one contains 342 fares, and one contains 159 fares. The Station Agent combines the contents of the three bags, and then removes 217 fares. 8.____
How many fares are left?

A. 556 B. 557 C. 568 D. 991

9. What is $367.20 + $510.00 + $402.80? 9.____

A. $1,276.90 B. $1,277.90 C. $1,279.00 D. $1,280.00

10. A Station Agent earns $9.18 per hour when he works a 40-hour week and is paid for overtime at time and a half for all time worked over 4 hours. How much money for overtime should he receive if he worked a 48-hour week? 10.____

A. $109.16 B. $109.28 C. $110.16 D. $110.36

Questions 11-14.

DIRECTIONS: Questions 11 through 14 are to be answered SOLELY on the basis of the information contained in the paragraphs below titled LOST PROPERTY.

LOST PROPERTY

Whenever a passenger delivers a lost article to a Station Agent on duty in a booth, the Station Agent will give the passenger a receipt, entering on the receipt a description of the lost article and the finder's name and address. Should a passenger try to give a lost article to a Station Department employee other than a Station Agent in a change booth, the employee will offer to escort the passenger to the nearest 24-hour booth so a receipt may be given by the Station Agent in the booth. If the passenger declines, the employee will accept the lost article without giving a receipt, and take the article to the nearest 24-hour booth.

All employees finding a lost article will bring it to the Station Agent in the nearest 24-hour booth. The Station Agent on duty in the 24-hour booth will give the employee a receipt for the article.

Each employee who receives lost property will be held responsible for it unless he produces a receipt for it from another employee. Should any lost property, after having been placed in the care of a Station Agent, disappear from a booth or be delivered to anyone without proper authority, the last employee who signed for the lost property will be held strictly accountable.

11. Which of the following is the FIRST thing a Station Agent on duty in a booth should do upon receiving a lost article from a passenger? 11.____

    A. Notify his supervisor.
    B. Find out the name of the owner of the article.
    C. Give a receipt to the passenger.
    D. Fill out a report on the incident.

12. Which of the following is the FIRST thing a cleaner working on a station platform should do if a passenger tries to give him a lost article? 12.____

    A. Give the passenger a receipt.
    B. Direct the passenger to the Lost Property Office.
    C. Offer to escort the passenger to the nearest 24-hour booth.
    D. Notify his supervisor.

13. Which of the following persons will be held accountable if a lost article disappears after it has been turned in to the Station Agent in the nearest 24-hour booth? 13.____

    A. person who found the lost article
    B. Station Agent in the nearest 24-hour booth
    C. supervisor in charge of the station
    D. last employee who signed a receipt for the lost article

14. A cleaner finds an umbrella on a platform of a station. Three passengers see him pick it up, and all three claim the umbrella. The first passenger says the umbrella had dropped out of her shopping bag. The second says he had just laid the umbrella down until he could find something in his briefcase. The third says the umbrella belongs to his wife who just boarded a subway train. 14.____
    Which of the following should the cleaner do? Give the umbrella to the

    A. passenger he finds most believable
    B. Station Agent in the nearest 24-hour booth and get a receipt
    C. Nearest Platform Conductor and get a receipt
    D. Station Agent in the nearest booth, or to the nearest Platform Conductor or Supervisor, and get a receipt

15. In checking a book of consecutively numbered Senior Citizen tickets, you find there are no tickets between number 13,383 and number 13,833. 15.____
    How many tickets are missing?

    A. 448 B. 449 C. 450 D. 451

16. What is the value of 73 quarters? 16.____

 A. $18.25 B. $18.50 C. $18.75 D. $19.00

17. What is the value of 173 nickels? 17.____

 A. $8.55 B. $8.65 C. $8.75 D. $8.85

18. If a turnstile counter shows 28,841 at 10:00 P.M., and 1,348 passengers passed through that turnstile between 4:00 P.M. and 10:00 P.M., what was the reading at 4:00 P.M.? 18.____

 A. 27,303 B. 27,393 C. 27,403 D. 27,493

19. If a turnstile counter shows 49,739 at 11:00 A.M., and 2,157 passengers pass through that turnstile during the next three hours, what will be the reading at 2:00 P.M.? 19.____

 A. 41,896 B. 51,887 C. 51,896 D. 51,897

Questions 20-22.

DIRECTIONS: Questions 20 through 22 are to be answered SOLELY on the basis of the information contained in the paragraphs below titled SENIOR CITIZEN AND HANDICAPPED PASSENGER REDUCED FARE PROGRAM.

SENIOR CITIZEN AND HANDICAPPED PASSENGER
REDUCED FARE PROGRAM

Upon display of his or her Medicare Card, Senior Citizen Reduced Fare Card, or Handicapped Photo I.D. Card to the Station Agent on duty, and upon purchase of a fare or evidence of having a fare, a passenger will be issued a free return trip ticket. The passenger will then be directed to deposit full fare in a turnstile and enter the controlled area. Return trip tickets are valid 24 hours a day, 7 days a week, for the day of purchase and the following two (2) calendar days.

Each return trip ticket will be stamped with the station name and the date only at the time of issuing to a properly identified Senior Citizen or handicapped passenger. Overstamping of tickets is not allowed. Return trip tickets issued from 2300 hours will be stamped with the date of the following day.

On the return trip, the Station Agent on duty will direct the passenger to enter the controlled are via the exit gate upon the passenger turning in the return trip ticket and displaying his or her Medicare Card, Senior Citizen Reduced Fare Card, or Handicapped Photo I.D. Card.

20. A Station Agent issued a free return ticket to a Senior Citizen who displayed a birth certificate and a fare.
The Station Agent's action was 20.____

 A. *proper* because the Station Agent had proof of the Senior Citizen's age
 B. *improper* because the Senior Citizen did not display a Medicare Card, Senior Citizen Reduced Fare Card or Handicapped Photo I.D. Card

C. *proper* because it is inconvenient for many Senior Citizens to obtain a Medicare Card, Senior Citizen Reduced Fare Card, or Handicapped Photo I.D. Card
D. *improper* because the Senior Citizen did not buy a fare from the Station Agent

21. The return trip ticket issued to a Senior Citizen is valid for ONLY 21.____

A. 24 hours
B. the day of purchase
C. two days
D. the day of purchase and the following two calendar days

22. A Station Agent denied entry to the controlled area via the exit gate to an 18-year-old handicapped passenger who turned in a correctly stamped return trip ticket, but did not display any type of identification card. 22.____
The Station Agent's action was

A. *proper* because the passenger should have displayed his Handicapped Photo I.D. Card
B. *improper* because the passenger turned in a correctly stamped return trip ticket
C. *proper* because the passenger should have displayed either his Handicapped Photo I.D. Card or Social Security Card
D. *improper* because it should have been obvious to the Station Agent that the passenger was handicapped

Questions 23-26.

DIRECTIONS: Questions 23 through 26 are to be answered by selecting the answer whose meaning is CLOSEST to the meaning of the underlined word in the sentence.

23. Station Agents must <u>ascertain</u> the identification of all individuals claiming to be Transit Authority employees. 23.____

A. observe B. record C. challenge D. verify

24. A Station Agent must not permit anyone to <u>loiter</u> near his booth. 24.____

A. throw refuse B. smoke
C. stand idly D. make noise

25. The Transit Authority has a program for eliminating <u>graffiti</u> in subway cars. 25.____

A. noise B. markings C. vandalism D. debris

26. The Station Agent will <u>deduct</u> the number of fares she sold from the number of fares she had in reserve when she started her tour of duty. 26.____

A. add B. subtract C. multiply D. divide

Questions 27-31.

DIRECTIONS: Questions 27 through 31 are to be answered SOLELY on the basis of the ASSIGNMENT SCHEDULE below. This schedule is similar to one used by Station Agents who have Lunch Relief tours. Station Agents on Lunch Relief tours take over the duties of other Station Agents so that they may go to lunch.

In addition, the Lunch Relief Clerk assists, retrieves fares from turnstiles, sells fares, watches gates, checks school passes, and escorts other Station Agents from one booth to another. The Lunch Relief Clerks must frequently refer to their schedules.

ASSIGNMENT SCHEDULE

JOB	TOUR	BOOTH HOURS	SAT.	SUN.	HOL
1233	Lunch Relief	(Mon. - Fri.) 7:30 AM - 3:30 PM	9AM - 5 PM	Same	Same

MONDAY - FRIDAY SCHEDULE

Duties	Station	Booth Number	Time Schedule
Sell Fares & Assist	Lexington Ave.	N306	7:30 - 9:20
Assist & Escort	42nd - 8th Ave.	N63toR147	9:30 - 9:40
Lunch Relief	7th Ave. E	N300	9:50 - 10:20
Escort	Lexington Ave.	N306 to N305	10:30 - 10:40
Lunch Relief	59th Street	R158	11:00 - 11:30
Lunch Relief	50th - 7th Ave.	R154	11:40 - 12:10
Lunch Relief	50th - 7th Ave.	R155	12:15 - 12:45
Lunch	Self	--	12:45 - 1:15
Assist & Escort	7th Ave. E	N300 to N301	1:35 - 2:05
Examine School Passes	59th - 7th Ave.	R158	2:25 - 3:30

SATURDAY SCHEDULE

Duties	Station	Booth Number	Time Schedule
Lunch Relief	50th - 8th Ave.	N56	9:00 - 9:30
Lunch Relief	50th - 8th Ave.	N57	9:35 - 10:05
Lunch Relief	50th - 7th Ave.	R154	10:15 - 10:45
Lunch Relief	50th - 7th Ave.	R155	10:50 - 11:20
Assist & Retrieve	42nd - 8th Ave.	N62	11:35 - 1:15
Assist & Retrieve	50th - 8th Ave.	N56	1:25 - 2:30
Lunch	Self	--	2:30 - 3:00
Assist & Sell Fares	50th - 8th Ave.	N56	3:10 - 5:00

SUN. & HOL. SCHEDULE

Same schedule as Saturday until 11:20 AM, then:

Duties	Station	Booth Number	Time Schedule
Lunch	Self	--	11:20 - 11:50
Assist & Retrieve	42nd - 8th Ave.	N62	12:00 - 12:50
Stand watch over gates	West 4th St.	N80	1:00 - 5:00

27. During which of the following periods does the Station Agent who has Lunch Relief Job 1233 have lunch on Thursdays? 27.____

A. 2:30-3:00
B. 6.11:00-11:30
C. 11:20-11:50
D. 0.12:45-1:15

28. At which station does the Station Agent who has Lunch Relief Job 1233 act ONLY as an escort? 28._____

A. West 4th Street
B. 42nd - 8th Ave.
C. Lexington Ave.
D. 7th Ave. E

29. Which of the following is one of the holiday duties of the Station Agent who has Lunch Relief Job 1233? 29._____

A. Assist and sell fares
B. Assist and retrieve
C. Lunch relief
D. Assist and escort

30. At which of the following booths does the Station Agent who has Lunch Relief Job 1233 work on Saturdays? 30._____

A. N63, N300, N301, N305
B. N56, N57, N62, N63, N80
C. N56, N57, N62, R154, R155
D. N56, N57, N62, R155, R158

31. During which of the following periods does the Station Agent who has Lunch Relief Job 1233 assist and retrieve on Sundays? 31._____

A. 11:35-1:15
B. 6.12:00-12:50
C. 0.1:25-2:30
D. 0.3:10-5:00

32. If a passenger hands you a twenty-dollar bill and asks for 7 fares, and you give him his change entirely in quarters, how many quarters should he receive? 32._____

A. 20 B. 12 C. 10 D. 8

33. If a passenger gives you 8 dollars and asks for 3 fares and for his change to be in nickels, how many nickels should you give him? 33._____

A. 10 B. 20 C. 25 D. 50

34. What is the sum of 2,513, 2,708 and 4,301? 34._____

A. 9,522 B. 9,523 C. 9,532 D. 9,533

35. What is the value of 3 half dollars, 11 quarters, 17 dimes, and 33 nickels? 35._____

A. $7.60 B. $7.75 C. $7.90 D. $8.05

36. In which borough is Grand Central Terminal located? 36._____

A. The Bronx
B. Brooklyn
C. Manhattan
D. Queens

37. In which borough is Forest Hills located? 37._____

A. The Bronx
B. Brooklyn
C. Staten Island
D. Queens

38. In which borough is Yankee Stadium located? 38._____

A. The Bronx
B. Brooklyn
C. Manhattan
D. Queens

39. In which borough is Flatbush Avenue located? 39.____

A. The Bronx B. Brooklyn
C. Manhattan D. Queens

40. Times Square is located at the intersection of Broadway, Sixth Avenue, and ______ Street. 40.____

A. 14th B. 23rd C. 34th D. 42nd

KEY (CORRECT ANSWERS)

1.	D	11.	C	21.	D	31.	B
2.	C	12.	C	22.	A	32.	C
3.	B	13.	D	23.	D	33.	A
4.	D	14.	B	24.	C	34.	A
5.	C	15.	B	25.	B	35.	A
6.	C	16.	A	26.	B	36.	C
7.	C	17.	B	27.	D	37.	D
8.	B	18.	D	28.	C	38.	A
9.	D	19.	C	29.	B/C	39.	B
10.	C	20.	B	30.	C	40.	D

READING COMPREHENSION
UNDERSTANDING AND INTERPRETING WRITTEN MATERIAL
EXAMINATION SECTION
TEST 1

DIRECTIONS Each question or incomplete statement is followed by several suggested answers or completions. Select the one that BEST answers the question or completes the statement. *PRINT THE LETTER OF THE CORRECT ANSWER IN THE SPACE AT THE RIGHT.*

Questions 1-8.

DIRECTIONS: Questions 1 through 8 are to be answered on the basis of the following regulations governing Newspaper Carriers when on subway trains or station platforms. These Newspaper Carriers are issued badges which entitle them to enter subway stations, when carrying papers in accordance with these regulations, without paying a fare.

REGULATIONS GOVERNING NEWSPAPER CARRIERS
WHEN ON SUBWAY TRAINS OR STATION PLATFORMS

1. Carriers must wear badges at all times when on trains.
2. Carriers must not sort, separate, or wrap bundles on trains or insert sections.
3. Carriers must not obstruct platform of cars or stations.
4. Carriers may make delivery to stands inside the stations by depositing their badge with the station agent.
5. Throwing of bundles is strictly prohibited and will be cause for arrest.
6. Each bundle must not be over 18" x 12" x 15".
7. Not more than two bundles shall be carried by each carrier. (An extra fare to be charged for a second bundle.)
8. No wire to be used on bundles carried into stations.

1. These regulations do NOT prohibit carriers on trains from _______ newspapers. 1._____

   A. sorting bundles of
   B. carrying bundles of
   C. wrapping bundles of
   D. inserting sections into

2. A carrier delivering newspapers to a stand inside of the station MUST 2._____

   A. wear his badge at all times
   B. leave his badge with the railroad clerk
   C. show his badge to the railroad clerk
   D. show his badge at the newsstand

3. Carriers are warned against throwing bundles of newspapers from trains MAINLY because these acts may 3._____

   A. wreck the stand
   B. cause injury to passengers
   C. hurt the carrier
   D. damage the newspaper

4. It is permissible for a carrier to temporarily leave his bundles of newspapers 4.____

A. near the subway car's door
B. at the foot of the station stairs
C. in front of the exit gate
D. on a station bench

5. Of the following, the carrier who should NOT be restricted from entering the subway is the one carrying a bundle which is ______long, ______ wide, and ______ high. 5.____

A. 15"; 18"; 18"
B. 18"; 12"; 18"
C. 18"; 12"; 15"
D. 18"; 15"; 15"

6. A carrier who will have to pay one fare is carrying ______ bundle(s). 6.____

A. one B. two C. three D. four

7. Wire may NOT be used for tying bundles because it may be 7.____

A. rusty
B. expensive
C. needed for other purposes
D. dangerous to other passengers

8. If a carrier is arrested in violation of these regulations, the PROBABLE reason is that he 8.____

A. carried too many papers
B. was not wearing his badge
C. separated bundles of newspapers on the train
D. tossed a bundle of newspapers to a carrier on a train

Questions 9-12.

DIRECTIONS: Questions 9 through 12 are to be answered on the basis of the Bulletin printed below. Read this Bulletin carefully before answering these questions. Select your answers ONLY on the basis of this Bulletin.

BULLETIN

Rule 107(m) states, in part, that *Before closing doors they (Conductors) must afford passengers an opportunity to detrain and entrain...*

Doors must be left open long enough to allow passengers to enter and exit from the train. Closing doors on passengers too quickly does not help to shorten the station stop and is a violation of the safety and courtesy which must be accorded to all our passengers.

The proper and effective way to keep passengers moving in and out of the train is to use the public address system. When the train is excessively crowded and passengers on the platform are pushing those in the cars, it may be necessary to close the doors after a reasonable period of time has been allowed.

Closing doors on passengers too quickly is a violation of rules and will be cause for disciplinary actions.

9. Which of the following statements is CORRECT about closing doors on passengers too quickly? It 9.____

   A. will shorten the running time from terminal to terminal
   B. shortens the station stop but is a violation of safety and courtesy
   C. does not help shorten the station stop time
   D. makes the passengers detrain and entrain quicker

10. The BEST way to get passengers to move in and out of cars quickly is to 10.____

   A. have the platform conductors urge passengers to move into doorways
   B. make announcements over the public address system
   C. start closing doors while passengers are getting on
   D. set a fixed time for stopping at each station

11. The conductor should leave doors open at each station stop long enough for passengers to 11.____

   A. squeeze into an excessively crowded train
   B. get from the local to the express train
   C. get off and get on the train
   D. hear the announcements over the public address system

12. Closing doors on passengers too quickly is a violation of rules and is cause for 12.____

   A. the conductor's immediate suspension
   B. the conductor to be sent back to the terminal for another assignment
   C. removal of the conductor at the next station
   D. disciplinary action to be taken against the conductor

Questions 13-15.

DIRECTIONS: Questions 13 through 15 are to be answered on the basis of the Bulletin printed below. Read this Bulletin carefully before answering these questions. Select your answers ONLY on the basis of this Bulletin.

<u>BULLETIN</u>

Conductors assigned to train service are not required to wear uniform caps from June 1 to September 30, inclusive.

Conductors assigned to platform duty are required to wear the uniform cap at all times. Conductors are reminded that they must furnish their badge numbers to anyone who requests same.

During the above-mentioned period, conductors may remove their uniform coats. The regulation summer short-sleeved shirts must be worn with the regulation uniform trousers. Suspenders are not permitted if the uniform coat is removed. Shoes are to be black but sandals, sneakers, suede, canvas, or two-tone footwear must not be worn.

Conductors may work without uniform tie if the uniform coat is removed. However, only the top collar button may be opened. The tie may not be removed if the uniform coat is worn.

13. Conductors assigned to platform duty are required to wear uniform caps 13.____

    A. at all times except from June 1 to September 30, inclusive
    B. whenever they are on duty
    C. only from June 1 to September 30, inclusive
    D. only when they remove their uniform coats

14. Suspenders are permitted ONLY if conductors wear 14.____

    A. summer short-sleeved shirts with uniform trousers
    B. uniform trousers without belt loops
    C. the type permitted by the authority
    D. uniform coats

15. A conductor MUST furnish his badge number to 15.____

    A. authority supervisors only
    B. members of special inspection only
    C. anyone who asks him for it
    D. passengers only

Questions 16-17.

DIRECTIONS: Questions 16 and 17 are to be answered SOLELY on the basis of the following Bulletin.

<u>BULLETIN</u>

Effective immediately, Conductors on trains equipped with public address systems shall make the following announcements in addition to their regular station announcement. At stations where passengers normally board trains from their homes or places of employment, the announcement shall be *Good Morning* or *Good Afternoon* or *Good Evening,* depending on the time of the day. At stations where passengers normally leave trains for their homes or places of employment, the announcement shall be *Have a Good Day* or *Good Night,* depending on the time of day or night.

16. The MAIN purpose of making the additional announcements mentioned in the Bulletin is MOST likely to 16.____

    A. keep passengers informed about the time of day
    B. determine whether the public address system works in case of an emergency
    C. make the passengers' ride more pleasant
    D. have the conductor get used to using the public address system

17. According to this Bulletin, a conductor should greet passengers boarding the *D* train at the Coney Island Station at 8 A.M. Monday by announcing 17.____

    A. Have a Good Day
    B. Good Morning
    C. Watch your step as you leave
    D. Good Evening

Questions 18-25.

DIRECTIONS: Questions 18 through 25 are to be answered on the basis of the information regarding the incident given below. Read this information carefully before answering these questions.

INCIDENT

As John Brown, a cleaner, was sweeping the subway station platform, in accordance with his assigned schedule, he was accused by Henry Adams of unnecessarily bumping him with the broom and scolded for doing this work when so many passengers were on the platform. Adams obtained Brown's badge number and stated that he would report the matter to the Transit Authority. Standing around and watching this were Mary Smith, a schoolteacher, Ann Jones, a student, and Joe Black, a maintainer, with Jim Roe, his helper, who had been working on one of the turnstiles. Brown thereupon proceeded to take the names and addresses of these people as required by the Transit Authority rule which directs that names and addresses of as many disinterested witnesses be taken as possible. Shortly thereafter, a train arrived at the station and Adams, as well as several other people, boarded the train and left. Brown went back to his work of sweeping the station.

18. The cleaner was sweeping the station at this time because 18.____

A. the platform was unusually dirty
B. there were very few passengers on the platform
C. he had no regard for the passengers
D. it was set by his work schedule

19. This incident proves that 19.____

A. witnesses are needed in such cases
B. porters are generally careless
C. subway employees stick together
D. brooms are dangerous in the subway

20. Joe Black was a 20.____

A. helper B. maintainer
C. cleaner D. teacher

21. The number of persons witnessing this incident was 21.____

A. 2 B. 3 C. 4 D. 5

22. The addresses of witnesses are required so that they may later be 22.____

A. depended on to testify B. recognized
C. paid D. located

23. The person who said he would report this incident to the transit authority was 23.____

A. Black B. Adams C. Brown D. Roe

24. The ONLY person of the following who positively did NOT board the train was 24.____

A. Brown B. Smith C. Adams D. Jones

25. As a result of this incident, 25.____

A. no action need be taken against the cleaner unless Adams makes a written complaint
B. the cleaner should be given the rest of the day off
C. the handles of the brooms used should be made shorter
D. Brown's badge number should be changed

KEY (CORRECT ANSWERS)

1. B
2. B
3. B
4. D
5. C

6. A
7. D
8. D
9. C
10. B

11. C
12. D
13. B
14. D
15. C

16. C
17. B
18. D
19. A
20. B

21. C
22. D
23. B
24. A
25. A

TEST 2

DIRECTIONS: Each question or incomplete statement is followed by several suggested answers or completions. Select the one that BEST answers the question or completes the statement. *PRINT THE LETTER OF THE CORRECT ANSWER IN THE SPACE AT THE RIGHT.*

Questions 1-10.

DIRECTIONS: Questions 1 through 10 are to be answered on the basis of the information contained in the following safety rules. Read the rules carefully before answering these questions.

SAFETY RULES

Employees must take every precaution to prevent accidents, or injury to persons, or damage to property. For this reason, they must observe conditions of the equipment and tools with which they work, and the structures upon which they work.

It is the duty of all employees to report to their superior all dangerous conditions which they may observe. Employees must use every precaution to prevent the origin of fire. If they discover smoke or a fire in the subway, they shall proceed to the nearest telephone and notify the trainmaster giving their name, badge number, and location of the trouble.

In case of accidents on the subway system, employees must, if possible, secure the name, address, and telephone number of any passengers who may have been injured.

Employees at or near the location of trouble on the subway system, whether it be a fire or an accident, shall render all practical assistance which they are qualified to perform.

1. The BEST way for employees to prevent an accident is to 1.____

   A. secure the names of the injured persons
   B. arrive promptly at the location of the accident
   C. give their name and badge numbers to the trainmaster
   D. take all necessary precautions

2. In case of trouble, trackmen are NOT expected to 2.____

   A. report fires
   B. give help if they don't know how
   C. secure telephone numbers of persons injured in subway accidents
   D. give their badge number to anyone

3. Trackmen MUST 3.____

   A. be present at all fires
   B. see all accidents
   C. report dangerous conditions
   D. be the first to discover smoke in the subway

4. Observing conditions means to 4.____

A. look at things carefully
B. report what you see
C. ignore things that are none of your business
D. correct dangerous conditions

5. A dangerous condition existing on the subway system which a trackman should observe and report to his superior would be 5.____

A. passengers crowding into trains
B. trains running behind schedule
C. tools in defective condition
D. some newspapers on the track

6. If a trackman discovers a badly worn rail, he should 6.____

A. not take any action
B. remove the worn section of rail
C. notify his superior
D. replace the rail

7. The MAIN reason a trackman should observe the condition of his tools is 7.____

A. so that they won't be stolen
B. because they don't belong to him
C. to prevent accidents
D. because they cannot be replaced

8. If a passenger who paid his fare is injured in a subway accident, it is MOST important that an employee obtain the passenger's 8.____

A. name
B. age
C. badge number
D. destination

9. An employee who happens to be at the scene of an accident on a crowded station of the system should 9.____

A. not give assistance unless he chooses to do so
B. leave the scene immediately
C. question all bystanders
D. render whatever assistance he can

10. If a trackman discovers a fire at one end of a station platform and telephones the information to the trainmaster, he need NOT give 10.____

A. the trainmaster's name
B. the name of the station involved
C. his own name
D. the number of his badge

Questions 11-15.

DIRECTIONS: Questions 11 through 15 are to be answered on the basis of the information contained in the safety regulations given below. Refer to these rules in answering these questions.

REGULATIONS FOR SMALL GROUPS WHO MOVE FROM POINT TO POINT ON THE TRACKS

Employees who perform duties on the tracks in small groups and who move from point to point along the trainway must be on the alert at all times and prepared to clear the track when a train approaches without unnecessarily slowing it down. Underground at all times, and out-of-doors between sunset and sunrise, such employees must not enter upon the tracks unless each of them is equipped with an approved light. Flashlights must not be used for protection by such groups. Upon clearing the track to permit a train to pass, each member of the group must give a proceed signal, by hand or light, to the motorman of the train. Whenever such small groups are working in an area protected by caution lights or flags, but are not members of the gang for whom the flagging protection was established, they must not give proceed signals to motormen. The purpose of this rule is to avoid a motorman's confusing such signal with that of the flagman who is protecting a gang. Whenever a small group is engaged in work of an engrossing nature or at any time when the view of approaching trains is limited by reason of curves or otherwise, one man of the group, equipped with a whistle, must be assigned properly to warn and protect the man or men at work and must not perform any other duties while so assigned.

11. If a small group of men are traveling along the tracks toward their work location and a train approaches, they should 11.____

    A. stop the train
    B. signal the motorman to go slowly
    C. clear the track
    D. stop immediately

12. Small groups may enter upon the tracks 12.____

    A. only between sunset and sunrise
    B. provided each has an approved light
    C. provided their foreman has a good flashlight
    D. provided each man has an approved flashlight

13. After a small group has cleared the tracks in an area unprotected by caution lights or flags, 13.____

    A. each member must give the proceed signal to the motorman
    B. the foreman signals the motorman to proceed
    C. the motorman can proceed provided he goes slowly
    D. the last member off the tracks gives the signal to the motorman

14. If a small group is working in an area protected by the signals of a track gang, the members of the small group 14.____

    A. need not be concerned with train movement
    B. must give the proceed signal together with the track gang

C. can delegate one of their members to give the proceed signal
D. must not give the proceed signal

15. If the view of approaching trains is blocked, the small group should 15.____

A. move to where they can see the trains
B. delegate one of the group to warn and protect them
C. keep their ears alert for approaching trains
D. refuse to work at such locations

Questions 16-25.

DIRECTIONS: Questions 16 through 25 are to be answered SOLELY on the basis of the article about general safety precautions given below.

GENERAL SAFETY PRECAUTIONS

When work is being done on or next to a track on which regular trains are running, special signals must be displayed as called for in the general rules for flagging. Yellow caution signals, green clear signals, and a flagman with a red danger signal are required for the protection of traffic and workmen in accordance with the standard flagging rules. The flagman shall also carry a white signal for display to the motorman when he may proceed. The foreman in charge must see that proper signals are displayed.

On elevated lines during daylight hours, the yellow signal shall be a yellow flag, the red signal shall be a red flag, the green signal shall be a green flag, and the white signal shall be a white flag. In subway sections, and on elevated lines after dark, the yellow signal shall be a yellow lantern, the red signal shall be a red lantern, the green signal shall be a green lantern, and the white signal shall be a white lantern.

Caution and clear signals are to be secured to the elevated or subway structure with non-metallic fastenings outside the clearance line of the train and on the motorman's side of the track.

16. On elevated lines during daylight hours, the caution signal is a 16.____

A. yellow lantern
B. green lantern
C. yellow flag
D. green flag

17. In subway sections, the clear signal is a 17.____

A. yellow lantern
B. green lantern
C. yellow flag
D. green flag

18. The MINIMUM number of lanterns that a subway track flagman should carry is 18.____

A. 1
B. 2
C. 3
D. 4

19. The PRIMARY purpose of flagging is to protect the 19.____

A. flagman
B. motorman
C. track workers
D. railroad

20. A suitable fastening for securing caution lights to the elevated or subway structure is 20.____

A. copper nails
B. steel wire
C. brass rods
D. cotton twine

21. On elevated structures during daylight hours, the red flag is held by the 21.____

A. motorman
B. foreman
C. trackman
D. flagman

22. The signal used in the subway to notify a motorman to proceed is a 22.____

A. white lantern
B. green lantern
C. red flag
D. yellow flag

23. The caution, clear, and danger signals are displayed for the information of 23.____

A. trackmen
B. workmen
C. flagmen
D. motormen

24. Since the motorman's cab is on the right-hand side, caution signals should be secured to the 24.____

A. right-hand running rail
B. left-hand running rail
C. structure to the right of the track
D. structure to the left of the track

25. In a track work gang, the person responsible for the proper display of signals is the 25.____

A. track worker
B. foreman
C. motorman
D. flagman

KEY (CORRECT ANSWERS)

1.	D	11.	C
2.	B	12.	B
3.	C	13.	A
4.	A	14.	D
5.	C	15.	B
6.	C	16.	C
7.	C	17.	B
8.	A	18.	B
9.	D	19.	C
10.	A	20.	D

21. D
22. A
23. D
24. C
25. B

TEST 3

DIRECTIONS: Each question or incomplete statement is followed by several suggested answers or completions. Select the one that BEST answers the question or completes the statement. *PRINT THE LETTER OF THE CORRECT ANSWER IN THE SPACE AT THE RIGHT.*

Questions 1-6.

DIRECTIONS: Questions 1 through 6 are to be answered on the basis of the Bulletin Order given below. Refer to this bulletin when answering these questions.

BULLETIN ORDER NO. 67

SUBJECT: Procedure for Handling Fire Occurrences

In order that the Fire Department may be notified of all fires, even those that have been extinguished by our own employees, any employee having knowledge of a fire must notify the Station Department Office immediately on telephone extensions D-4177, D-4181, D-4185, or D-4189.

Specific information regarding the fire should include the location of the fire, the approximate distance north or south of the nearest station, and the track designation, line, and division.

In addition, the report should contain information as to the status of the fire and whether our forces have extinguished it or if Fire Department equipment is required.

When all information has been obtained, the Station Supervisor in Charge in the Station Department Office will notify the Desk Trainmaster of the Division involved.

Richard Roe,
Superintendent

1. An employee having knowledge of a fire should FIRST notify the 1.____

   A. Station Department Office
   B. Fire Department
   C. Desk Trainmaster
   D. Station Supervisor

2. If bulletin order number 1 was issued on January 2, bulletins are being issued at the monthly average of 2.____

   A. 8 B. 10 C. 12 D. 14

3. It is clear from the bulletin that 3.____

   A. employees are expected to be expert fire fighters
   B. many fires occur on the transit system
   C. train service is usually suspended whenever a fire occurs
   D. some fires are extinguished without the help of the Fire Department

4. From the information furnished in this bulletin, it can be assumed that the 4.____

   A. Station Department office handles a considerable number of telephone calls
   B. Superintendent Investigates the handling of all subway fires
   C. Fire Department is notified only in ease of large fires
   D. employee first having knowledge of the fire must call all 4 extensions

5. The PROBABLE reason for notifying the Fire Department even when the fire has been extinguished by a subway employee is because the Fire Department is 5.____

   A. a city agency
   B. still responsible to check the fire
   C. concerned with fire prevention
   D. required to clean up after the fire

6. Information about the fire NOT specifically required is 6.____

   A. track B. time of day C. station D. division

Questions 7-10.

DIRECTIONS: Questions 7 through 10 are to be answered on the basis of the paragraph on fire fighting shown below. When answering these questions, refer to this paragraph.

FIRE FIGHTING

A security officer should remember the cardinal rule that water or soda acid fire extinguishers should not be used on any electrical fire, and apply it in the case of a fire near the third rail. In addition, security officers should familiarize themselves with all available fire alarms and fire-fighting equipment within their assigned posts. Use of the fire alarm should bring responding Fire Department apparatus quickly to the scene. Familiarity with the fire-fighting equipment near his post would help in putting out incipient fires. Any man calling for the Fire Department should remain outside so that he can direct the Fire Department to the fire. As soon as possible thereafter, the special inspection desk must be notified, and a complete written report of the fire, no matter how small, must be submitted to this office. The security officer must give the exact time and place it started, who discovered it, how it was extinguished, the damage done, cause of same, list of any injured persons with the extent of their injuries, and the name of the Fire Chief in charge. All defects noticed by the security officer concerning the fire alarm or any fire-fighting equipment must be reported to the special inspection department.

7. It would be PROPER to use water to put out a fire in a(n) 7.____

   A. electric motor
   B. electric switch box
   C. waste paper trash can
   D. electric generator

8. After calling the Fire Department from a street box to report a fire, the security officer should then 8.____

   A. return to the fire and help put it out
   B. stay outside and direct the Fire Department to the fire
   C. find a phone and call his boss
   D. write out a report for the special inspection desk

9. A security officer is required to submit a complete written report of a fire 9._____

A. two weeks after the fire
B. the day following the fire
C. as soon as possible
D. at his convenience

10. In his report of a fire, it is NOT necessary for the security officer to state 10._____

A. time and place of the fire
B. who discovered the fire
C. the names of persons injured
D. quantity of Fire Department equipment used

Questions 11-16.

DIRECTIONS: Questions 11 through 16 are to be answered on the basis of the Notice given below. Refer to this Notice in answering these questions.

NOTICE

Your attention is called to Route Request Buttons that are installed on all new type Interlocking Home Signals where there is a choice of route in the midtown area. The route request button is to be operated by the motorman when the home signal is at danger and no call-on is displayed or when improper route is displayed.

To operate, the motorman will press the button for the desiredroute as indicated under each button; a light will then go on over the buttons to inform the motorman that his request has been registered in the tower.

If the towerman desires to give the motorman a route other than the one he selected, the towerman will cancel out the light over the route selection buttons. The motorman will then accept the route given.

If no route or call-on is given, the motorman will sound his whistle for the signal maintainer, secure his train, and call the desk trainmaster.

11. The official titles of the two classes of employee whose actions would MOST frequently be affected by the contents of this notice are 11._____

A. motorman and trainmaster
B. signal maintainer and trainmaster
C. towerman and motorman
D. signal maintainer and towerman

12. A motorman should use a route request button when 12._____

A. the signal indicates proceed on main line
B. a call-on is displayed
C. the signal indicates stop
D. the signal indicates proceed on diverging route

13. The PROPER way to request a route is to 13.____

A. press the button corresponding to the desired route
B. press the button a number of times to correspond with the number of the route requested
C. stop at the signal and blow four short blasts
D. stop at the signal and telephone the tower

14. The motorman will know that his requested route has been registered in the tower if 14.____

A. a light comes on over the route request buttons
B. an acknowledging signal is sounded on the tower horn
C. the light in the route request button goes dark
D. the home signal continues to indicate stop

15. Under certain conditions, when stopped at such home signal, the motorman must signal for a signal maintainer and call the desk trainmaster. 15.____
Such condition exists when, after standing awhile,

A. the towerman continues to give the wrong route
B. the towerman does not acknowledge the signal
C. no route or call-on is given
D. the light over the route request buttons is cancelled out

16. It is clear that route request buttons 16.____

A. eliminate train delays due to signals at junctions
B. keep the towerman alert
C. force motormen and towermen to be more careful
D. are a more accurate form of communication than the whistle.

Questions 17-22.

DIRECTIONS: Questions 17 through 22 are to be answered on the basis of the instructions for removal of paper given below. Read these instructions carefully before answering these questions.

GENERAL INSTRUCTIONS FOR REMOVAL OF PAPER

When a cleaner's work schedule calls for the bagging of paper, he will remove paper from the waste paper receptacles, bag it, and place the bags at the head end of the platform, where they will be picked up by the work train. He will fill bags with paper to a weight that can be carried without danger of personal injury, as porters are forbidden to drag bags of paper over the platform. Cleaners are responsible that all bags of paper are arranged so as to prevent their falling from the platform to tracks, and so as to not interfere with passenger traffic.

17. A GOOD reason for removing the paper from receptacles and placing it in bags is that bags are more easily 17.____

A. stored B. weighed C. handled D. emptied

18. The *head end* of a local station platform is the end 18.____

A. in the direction that trains are running
B. nearest to which the trains stop
C. where there is an underpass to the other side
D. at which the change booth is located

19. The MOST likely reason for having the filled bags placed at the head end of the station rather than at the other end is that 19.____

A. a special storage space is provided there for them
B. this end of the platform is farthest from the passengers
C. most porters' closets are located near the head end
D. the work train stops at this end to pick them up

20. Limiting the weight to which the bags can be filled is PROBABLY done to 20.____

A. avoid having too many ripped or broken bags
B. protect the porter against possible rupture
C. make sure that all bags are filled fairly evenly
D. insure that, when stored, the bags will not fall to the track

21. The MOST important reason for not allowing filled bags to be dragged over the platform is that the bags 21.____

A. could otherwise be loaded too heavily
B. might leave streaks on the platform
C. would wear out too quickly
D. might spill paper on the platform

22. The instructions do NOT hold a porter responsible for a bag of paper which 22.____

A. is torn due to dragging over a platform
B. falls on a passenger because it was poorly stacked
C. falls to the track without being pushed
D. is ripped open by school children

Questions 23-25.

DIRECTIONS: Questions 23 through 25 are to be answered on the basis of the situation described below. Consider the facts given in this situation when answering these questions.

SITUATION

A new detergent that is to be added to water and the resulting mixture just wiped on any surface has been tested by the station department and appeared to be excellent. However, you notice, after inspecting a large number of stations that your porters have cleaned with this detergent, that the surfaces cleaned are not as clean as they formerly were when the old method was used.

23. The MAIN reason for the station department testing the new detergent in the first place was to make certain that 23.____

    A. it was very simple to use
    B. a little bit would go a long way
    C. there was no stronger detergent on the market
    D. it was superior to anything formerly used

24. The MAIN reason that such a poor cleaning job resulted was MOST likely due to the 24.____

    A. porters being lax on the job
    B. detergent not being as good as expected
    C. incorrect amount of water being mixed with the detergent
    D. fact that the surfaces cleaned needed to be scrubbed

25. The reason for inspecting a number of stations was to 25.____

    A. determine whether all porters did the same job
    B. insure that the result of the cleaning job was the same in each location
    C. be certain that the detergent was used in each station inspected
    D. see whether certain surfaces cleaned better than others

---

KEY (CORRECT ANSWERS)

1. A
2. C
3. D
4. A
5. C
6. B
7. C
8. B
9. C
10. D
11. C
12. C
13. A
14. A
15. C
16. D
17. C
18. A
19. D
20. B
21. C
22. D
23. D
24. B
25. B

ARITHMETICAL REASONING

EXAMINATION SECTION
TEST 1

DIRECTIONS: Each question or incomplete statement is followed by several suggested answers or completions. Select the one that BEST answers the question or completes the statement. *PRINT THE LETTER OF THE CORRECT ANSWER IN THE SPACE AT THE RIGHT.*

Questions 1-7.

DIRECTIONS: In answering Questions 1 throuh 7, assume that a fare is worth $2.50.

1. A passenger gives you 3 one-dollar bills and asks for 1 fare. You should give the passenger 1 fare and ______ cents in change. 1.____

   A. 50 B. 40 C. 20 D. 15

2. If a passenger wants to get 4 fares without getting any change, he should give you EXACTLY 2.____

   A. $5.50 B. $7.50 C. $8.00 D. $10.00

3. The GREATEST number of fares that can be purchased by a passenger who gives you 6 quarters, 8 dimes, and 5 nickels is 3.____

   A. 0 B. 1 C. 2 D. 3

4. The TOTAL amount of money represented by 7 half-dollars, 12 quarters, 16 dimes, and 14 nickels is 4.____

   A. $7.80 B. $8.60 C. $8.70 D. $8.80

5. If a passenger wants to get 3 fares without getting any change, he should give you EXACTLY 5.____

   A. $6.00 B. $7.50 C. $8.00 D. $8.50

6. A passenger gives you a ten-dollar bill and asks for 3 fares. You should give the passenger 3 fares and ______ in change. 6.____

   A. $2.00 B. $2.25 C. $2.50 D. $5.00

7. The GREATEST number of fares that can be purchased by a passenger who gives you $6.65 is 7.____

   A. 2 B. 3 C. 4 D. 5

8. A car cleaner earns $11.00 an hour and works 8 hours a day, 5 days a week. In one week he would earn 8.____

   A. $180 B. $400 C. $420 D. $440

9. Suppose a cleaner uses daily 1 pound of soap when working in a car shop and 1/2 pound of soap when working in a terminal. In order to have enough soap for 7 days' work in the shop and 5 days' work in the terminal, the TOTAL number of pounds of soap required is 9.____

A. 6 B. 8 1/2 C. 9 1/2 D. 12

10. In mixing 10 gallons of cleaning solution, 21/2 pounds of soap are required. To mix 5 gallons of cleaning solution, the number of pounds of soap required is 10.____

A. 1 B. 1 1/2 C. 1 1/2 D. 2

11. A cleaner is given 5 pounds of soap and instructed to divide it into a number of 10-ounce containers. (There are 16 ounces in one pound.) The TOTAL number of such containers he should fill is 11.____

A. 5 B. 8 C. 10 D. 13

12. The sum of the following numbers, 3, 9, 7, 8, 6, 5, 2, is 12.____

A. between 35 and 39
B. more than 42
C. equal to 40
D. greater than 40

13. Suppose a gang of cleaners takes about one week to completely wash a large station. If there are four gangs at work, the number of such large stations that can be completely washed in five weeks is 13.____

A. 5 B. 12 C. 20 D. 25

14. If a cleaner can wash a wall 60 feet long and 15 feet high in a day, the TOTAL area, in square feet, he can wash in a day is 14.____

A. 450 B. 720 C. 900 D. 1,000

15. Thirty-eight passengers can be seated in a certain car, and 4 times that many can find standing room. The TOTAL passenger capacity of the car is 15.____

A. 190 B. 180 C. 152 D. 114

16. A cleaner works 8 hours a day, 5 days a week, at $11.17 an hour. In one week he will earn 16.____

A. $409.20 B. $446.80 C. $404.70 D. $400.40

17. The weekly pay for 8 hours a day, 5 days a week, at $14.685 an hour can be calculated as follows: 17.____

A. $14.865 x 8 + 5
B. $14.865 x 8 x 5
C. 8 x 5 x $14.685
D. 8 + 5 x $14.685

18. A gang of cleaners can completely wash a large subway station in a five-day work week. If there are four such gangs at work, the number of stations that can be washed in six weeks is 18.____

A. 15 B. 20 C. 24 D. 30

19. If a cleaner can wash a wall 75 feet long and 10 feet high in a day, the TOTAL area, in square feet, he can wash in a day is 19.____

A. 9,000 B. 750 C. 85 D. 65

Questions 20-25.

DIRECTIONS: Questions 20 through 25, inclusive, in Column I are questions of simple arithmetic, each of which has one of the answers listed in Column II. For each item in Column I, select the PROPER answer from Column II.

	COLUMN I	COLUMN II	
20.	1,585 plus 284	A. 1,285	20.____
21.	1,100 plus 98 plus 87	B. 1,304	21.____
22.	1,891 minus 587	C. 2,475	22.____
23.	275 times 9	D. 1,869	23.____
24.	53 times 7 times 5	E. 1,209	24.____
25.	8,463 divided by 7	F. 1,855	25.____

KEY (CORRECT ANSWERS)

1.	A	11.	B
2.	D	12.	C
3.	B	13.	C
4.	D	14.	C
5.	B	15.	A
6.	C	16.	B
7.	A	17.	C
8.	D	18.	C
9.	C	19.	B
10.	B	20.	D

21. A
22. B
23. C
24. F
25. E

SOLUTIONS TO PROBLEMS

1. $3.00 - $2.50 = $.50 change
2. (4)($2.50) = $10.00
3. (6)(.25) + (8)(.10) + (5)(.05) = $2.55, which is 1 fare
4. (7)(.50) + (12)(.25) + (16)(.10) + (14)(.05) = $8.80
5. (3)($2.50) = $7.50
6. $10- (3)($2.50) = $2.50 change
7. $6.05 ÷ $2.50 = 2.66, so 2 is the maximum number of fares
8. ($11)(8)(5) = $440
9. (7)(1 lb.) + (5)(1/2 lb.) = 91/2 lbs.
10. (2 1/2)(5/10) = 1 1/4 lbs.
11. (5)(16) ÷ 10 = 8 containers
12. 3 + 9 + 7 + 8 + 6 + 5 + 2 = 40
13. Four gangs can wash 4 stations in 1 week. Thus, in 5 weeks they will do (4)(5) = 20 stations.
14. (60 ft.)(15 ft.) = 900 sq.ft.
15. Total capacity = 38 + 4(38) = 190 passengers
16. ($11.17)(8)(5) = $446.80
17. Weekly pay = (8)(5)($14.685)
18. Six weeks = 6 gang-weeks. Then, (4)(6) = 24 stations
19. (75 ft.)(10 ft.) = 750 sq.ft.
20. 1585 + 284 = 1869
21. 1100 + 98 + 87 = 1285
22. 1891 - 587 = 1304
23. (275)(9) = 2475
24. (53)(7)(5) = 1855
25. 8463 ÷ 7 = 1209

TEST 2

DIRECTIONS: Each question or incomplete statement is followed by several suggested answers or completions. Select the one that BEST answers the question or completes the statement. *PRINT THE LETTER OF THE CORRECT ANSWER IN THE SPACE AT THE RIGHT.*

Questions 1-10.

DIRECTIONS: Questions 1 through 10 inclusive are based ONLY on the information contained in the List of Cleaning Supplies given below. Read this list carefully before answering these questions.

LIST OF CLEANING SUPPLIES

Lemon Oil	-1 quart for two weeks
Disinfectant	-1/2 gallon per week
Pumice Powder	-15 lbs. always on hand
Metal Polish	-1 quart for two weeks
Toilet Paper	-10 to 20 packages per week for an average station
Soap Powder	-10 to 15 lbs. per week for an average station and 20 to 25 lbs. per week for a large station

1. The quantity of lemon oil required per week is 1.____

   A. 1/2 quart B. 1 quart C. 2 quarts D. 1 gallon

2. The EXACT quantity of pumice powder required per week is ______ pounds. 2.____

   A. 10 B. 15 C. 20 D. not given

3. The MAXIMUM total amount of soap powder required in one week for one average station and one large station is ______ pounds. 3.____

   A. 40 B. 30 C. 25 D. 15

4. The quantity of disinfectant required every two weeks is 4.____

   A. 1 quart B. 2 quarts C. 3/4 gallon D. 1 gallon

5. An average station is definitely specified for the issue of 5.____

   A. toilet paper
   B. disinfectant
   C. lemon oil
   D. pumice

6. The LEAST amount of soap powder required per week for a large station is ______ pounds. 6.____

   A. 25 B. 20 C. 14 D. 10

7. The two items which are supplied in equal quantities are lemon oil and 7.____

   A. metal polish
   B. soap powder
   C. disinfectant
   D. pumice

8. The TOTAL quantity of disinfectant, lemon oil, and metal polish required every two weeks is _______ gallon(s). 8._____

A. 1 1/2 B. 1 C. 3/4 D. 1/2

9. The MAXIMUM amount of soap powder required every two weeks at an average station is _______ pounds. 9._____

A. 15 B. 20 C. 30 D. 50

10. The quantity of toilet paper required is given in number of 10._____

A. packages B. rolls C. pounds D. feet

11. If a half pound of soap powder is required to clean 200 square feet of tile, then the number of pounds of soap required to clean 900 square feet of tile is 11._____

A. 1 3/4 B. 2 C. 21/4 D. 21/2

Questions 12-17.

DIRECTIONS: In answering Questions 12 through 17, assume that a fare is worth $2.50.

12. The GREATEST number of fares that can be purchased by a passenger who gives you 6 one-dollar bills is 12._____

A. 2 B. 3 C. 4 D. 5

13. If a passenger wants to get 2 fares without getting any change, he should give you EXACTLY 13._____

A. $2.50 B. $4.00 C. $5.00 D. $6.00

14. A passenger gives you a $20 bill and asks for 3 fares. You should give the passenger 3 fares and _______ in change. 14._____

A. $10.00 B. $12.50 C. $15.00 D. $15.50

15. The GREATEST number of fares that can be purchased by a passenger who gives you 15 quarters, 10 dimes, and 10 nickels is 15._____

A. 0 B. 1 C. 2 D. 3

16. If a passenger wants to get 2 fares without getting any change, he should give you _______ quarters, _______ dime(s), and _______ nickel(s). 16._____

A. 10; 10; 6
B. 12; 11; 18
C. 8; 10; 9
D. 9; 12; 11

17. After you have been in the booth for 10 minutes, you find that you have collected a total of 1 five-dollar bill, 6 one-dollar bills, 4 half-dollars, 16 quarters, 32 dimes, and 30 nickels.
The TOTAL amount of money that you have collected is 17._____

A. $18.20 B. $19.50 C. $20.55 D. $21.70

18. The weekly pay of a clerk for 8 hours a day, 5 days a week, at $15.09 an hour is 18._____

A. $591.60 B. $603.60 C. $636.00 D. $639.60

Questions 19-25.

DIRECTIONS: Questions 19 through 25, inclusive, in Column I are questions of simple arithmetic, each of which has one of the answers listed in Column II. For each item in Column I, select the PROPER answer from Column II.

	COLUMN I	COLUMN II	
19.	659 plus 1,609	A. 1,268	19.____
20.	252 times 9	B. 1,508	20.____
21.	9,072 divided by 4	C. 2,128	21.____
22.	1,357 plus 89 plus 62	D. 2,268	22.____
23.	76 times 4 times 7	E. 2,508	23.____
24.	8,876 divided by 7		24.____
25.	2,205 minus 697		25.____

KEY (CORRECT ANSWERS)

1. A
2. D
3. A
4. D
5. A

6. B
7. A
8. A
9. C
10. A

11. C
12. A
13. C
14. B
15. C

16. B
17. D
18. B
19. D
20. D

21. D
22. B
23. C
24. A
25. B

SOLUTIONS TO PROBLEMS

1. 1÷ 2 = 1/2 quart per week
2. The amount of pumice powder required per week is unknown.
3. 15 + 25 = 40 lbs. maximum
4. (1/2)(2) = 1 gallon per 2 weeks
5. The use of toilet paper is specifically quantified for an average station.
6. 20 lbs. of soap powder is the minimum needed per week for a large station.
7. Lemon oil and metal polish are both listed as 1 quart for 2 weeks.
8. (1/2)(2) + (1/4)(1) + (1/4)(1) = 1 1/2 gallons per 2 weeks
9. (15)(2) = 30 lbs. maximum for 2 weeks for an average station
10. Toilet paper quantity is given in packages.
11. 1 lb. is needed for 400 sq.ft., so 900/400 = 2 1/4 lbs. are needed for 900 sq.ft. of tile.
12. $6.00 ÷ $2.50 = 2 fares and $1.00 change
13. (2)($2.50) = $5.00
14. $ 20 - (3)($2.50) = $12.50 change
15. (15)(25) + (10)(.10) + (10)(.05) = $5.25. Then, $5.25 ÷ $2.50 = 2 fares and $.25 change.
16. 2 fares = $5.00 = 12 quarters, 11 dimes, and 18 nickels
17. (1)($5.00) + (6)($1.00) + (4)(.50) + (16)(.25) + (32)(.10) + (30)(.05) = $21.70
18. ($15.09)(8)(5) = $603.60
19. 659 + 1609 = 2268
20. (252)(9) = 2268
21. 9072 ÷ 4 = 2268
22. 1357 + 89 + 62 = 1508
23. (76)(4)(7) = 2128
24. 8876 ÷ 7 = 1268
25. 2205 - 697 = 1508

TEST 3

DIRECTIONS: Each question or incomplete statement is followed by several suggested answers or completions. Select the one that BEST answers the question or completes the answer. *PRINT THE LETTER OF THE CORRECT ANSWER IN THE SPACE AT THE RIGHT.*

1. Six cleaners can clean a certain tile wall in 3 hours. If two of the cleaners left one hour after starting work, the job would require ______ hours. 1.____

   A. 3 1/2 B. 4 C. 5 D. 9

2. Ten car trains arrive on five minute intervals at a terminal station. 2.____
   Assuming that each car carries 120 passengers, the number of passengers exiting from the station in an hour is NEAREST to

   A. 8,200 B. 12,000 C. 14,400 D. 16,000

3. A station having a total platform area of 22,575 sq. ft. is to be swept twice a week. 3.____
   If the average area that can be swept per hour is 5,250 sq. ft., the total time to be allotted for the twice-weekly sweeping is CLOSEST to ______ hours ______ minutes.

   A. 4; 6 B. 4; 18 C. 8; 36 D. 9; 20

4. For three adjacent stations for the same period, the first requires twice as much sawdust as the second and the second twice as much as the third. 4.____
   If 14 bags of sawdust are to be properly distributed to these stations, the first station should receive ______ bags.

   A. 4 B. 6 C. 8 D. 10

5. A railroad clerk, paid $10.80 an hour, works a 7:00 A.M. to 3:00 P.M. tour of duty Monday through Friday. 5.____
   What is his gross pay for a particular day on which he is required to attend a class on a new station department procedure for two hours after the completion of his tour of duty? (Assume time and a half over 40 hours a week.)

   A. $86.40 B. $108.00 C. $118.80 D. $129.60

6. When formulating the annual operating budget in the station department, it is necessary to determine the number of man-days required to cover the various work programs. 6.____
   If the railroad cleaner's work program calls for 2,354 daily tours, 2,163 Saturday tours, and 1,980 Sunday tours (including holidays), then the number of man-days which are normally required to cover this one-year work program without taking into account vacation coverage is MOST NEARLY

   A. 730,000 B. 780,000 C. 830,000 D. 880,000

7. A railroad clerk, paid $11.48 an hour, works a 7:00 A.M. to 3:00 P.M. tour of duty Monday through Friday. 7.____
   What is his gross pay for a particular week if he is ordered to instruct a newly-appointed railroad clerk in the performance of his duties in his booth each day of that week during his tour? (Total 3 1/3 overtime hours.)

   A. $482.16 B. $516.60 C. $533.82 D. $539.56

8. If the total number of accidents to the public on authority property in May 2014 was 529 and in May 2015 was 585, the percent increase in accidents in May 2015 as compared to May 2014 is CLOSEST to 8.____

A. 7% B. 9% C. 11 % D. 13%

9. Assume that 326 railroad cleaners will begin using a new type of disinfectant at certain stations as part of a test to determine the suitability of the disinfectant for authority use. If 1 1/2 ounces of undiluted disinfectant must be added to 3 gallons of water to make a satisfactory solution of the disinfectant and each cleaner is expected to use approximately 5 gallons of disinfectant solution each week, the amount of undiluted disinfectant needed for ALL the cleaners for a 6-week test is ______ ounces. 9.____

A. 3,890 B. 4,890 C. 4,990 D. 5,890

10. On a particular line, the station platforms are 600 feet in length. The MAXIMUM number of proposed new 75-foot long cars that a train on this line may have is ______ cars. 10.____

A. 10 B. 8 C. 6 D. 4

11. If the distance between two terminals is 11.4 miles, then a train which has made 5 roundtrips has traveled MOST NEARLY ______ miles. 11.____

A. 141 B. 114 C. 100 D. 57

12. A railroad cleaner works on the 4:00 P.M. to 12:00 Midnight shift and is paid at the hourly rate of $7.36. Assuming that he does not work overtime, his regular weekly pay is 12.____

A. $297.10 B. $296.80 C. $296.20 D. $294.40

13. If 15 trains per hour are operated on a certain track, the average headway is MOST NEARLY ______ minutes. 13.____

A. 6 B. 5 C. 4 D. 3

14. Twelve trains, consisting of 8 cars each, arrive at a terminal station at intervals of 10 minutes. Assuming that each car carries 135 passengers, the total number of passengers exiting from the 12 trains is NEAREST to 14.____

A. 16,200 B. 12,960 C. 10,800 D. 6,480

15. Six cleaners can clean a certain tile wall in 4 hours. If 3 of the cleaners leave two hours after starting work, the job would require a TOTAL time closest to ______ hours. 15.____

A. 10 B. 8 C. 6 D. 4

16. Assuming that 4 dimes weigh one ounce, then 1,000 dimes will weigh CLOSEST to a total of ______ pounds. 16.____

A. 15.6 B. 14.0 C. 12.5 D. 9.2

17. A cleaner works a regular work week of 40 hours and is paid at the rate of $7.16 per hour. Allowing 20% for all deductions from his gross pay, his take-home pay is 17.____

A. $343.68 B. $296.40 C. $229.12 D. $214.80

18. When 40% of 1,400 is subtracted from 2,100, the answer is 18.____

A. 2,044 B. 1,700 C. 1,540 D. 1,260

19. A detergent that is used in cleaning must be mixed with the correct amount of water to be effective. Assuming that the instructions state that 1 1/2 ounces of detergent should be mixed with each gallon of water, then the amount of detergent that must be used for a pail containing 2 1/2 gallons of water is CLOSEST to ______ ounces. 19.____

A. 37.5 B. 25 C. 3.75 D. 2.5

20. Two walls in a station are to be cleaned. One wall is 63 feet long and 7.5 feet high, and the other wall is 46 feet long and 9 feet high.
The total wall area, in square feet, to be cleaned is CLOSEST to 20.____

A. 981 B. 886.5 C. 817.5 D. 125.5

21. 10 cars must be cleaned with detergent that costs $6.00 a gallon.
If each car requires 6 gallons, the total cost will be 21.____

A. $180 B. $240 C. $300 D. $360

22. The answer to 2/5 x 0.85 is 22.____

A. 3.4 B. 1.7 C. 0.34 D. 0.17

23. A certain job takes 6 maintainers a total of 12 working days to complete provided they each work 2 hours of overtime each day.
How many maintainers should be assigned to this identical job if it is to be done in 18 working days without any overtime? (Assume that the actual number of hours a maintainer works in a day without overtime is 8 hours, and assume that all of them work at the same rate of speed.) 23.____

A. 4 B. 5 C. 6 D. 7

24. A passenger asks for 3 fares and hands the railroad clerk 10 dollars.
Since fares cost $2.50 each, the SMALLEST number of coins the passenger can be given in change is 24.____

A. 0 B. 1 C. 2 D. 3

25. In a given station, if there are twice as many paid passengers on Thursday as on Saturday, and one-half as many on Sunday as on Saturday, it follows that the number on Sunday is ______ as many as on Thursday. 25.____

A. four times
B. twice
C. one-half
D. one-quarter

KEY (CORRECT ANSWERS)

1. B
2. C
3. C
4. C
5. C

6. C
7. B
8. C
9. B
10. B

11. B
12. D
13. C
14. B
15. C

16. A
17. C
18. C
19. C
20. B

21. D
22. C
23. B
24. B
25. D

SOLUTIONS TO PROBLEMS

1. (6)(3) = 18 man-hours. After 6 man-hours are completed, only 4 cleaners are left. Then, (18-6) ÷ 4=3 additional hours will be needed. Thus, a total of 3 + 1 = 4 hours are needed to do the entire job. (Note: 6 man-hours = 6 men 1 hour) 1.____
2. (120)(60/5)(10) = 14,400 passengers 2.____
3. (2)(22,575) ÷ 5250 = 8.6 hours = 8 hours, 36 minutes 3.____
4. Let 4x, 2x, x represent the amount of sawdust for the 1st, 2nd, 3rd stations, respectively. Then, 4x + 2x + x = 14. Solving, x = 2. Then, the 1st station receives (4) (2) = 8 bags. 4.____
5. (8)($10.80) + (2)($16.20) = $118.80 5.____
6. Unable to complete. Insufficient information. 6.____
7. ($11.48)(40) + ($17.22(3 1/3) = $516.60 7.____
8. (585-529) ÷ 529 ≈ 11% increase 8.____
9. (326)(5)(6) = 9780 gallons of water. Then, the amount of disinfectant needed = (9780)(l1/2) ÷ 3 = 4890 ounces. 9.____
10. 600 ÷ 75 = 8 cars maximum 10.____
11. (11.4)(2)(5) = 114 miles (Note: Each roundtrip = (11.4)(2) = 22.8 miles) 11.____
12. ($7.36)(8)(5) = $294.40 12.____
13. 60 15 = 4 minutes 13.____
14. (12)(8)(135) = 12,960 passengers 14.____
15. (6)(4) = 24 man-hours. Since (6)(2) = 12 man-hours, there are 12 man-hours left for 3 cleaners. 12 ÷ 3 = 4 additional hours to finish the job. Now, 2 + 4 = 6 hours total are required. 15.____
16. 1000 ÷ 4 = 250 oz. ≈15.6 lbs. 16.____
17. Take-home pay = ($7.16)(40)(.80) = $229.12 17.____
18. 2100 - (.40)(1400) = 1540 18.____
19. (1 1/2)(2 1/2) = 3.75 oz. 19.____
20. (63)(7.5) + (46)(9) =886.5 sq.ft. 20.____
21. Each can 6 gallons x $6.00 = $36. 36 x 10 cans = $360 21.____
22. (2/5)(.85) = (.40)(.85) = .34 22.____
23. (6)(12)(10) = 720 man-hours. 18 working days with no overtime = (18)(8) = 144 hours. Finally, 720 ÷ 144 = 5 maintainers are needed. 23.____

24. \$10 - (3)(\$2.50) = \$2.50 The smallest number of coins for \$2.50 is one half-dollar 24._____

25. Let x = passengers on Saturday. Then, x/2 and 2x represent the number of passengers on Sunday and Thursday, respectively. 25._____
Finally, x/2 ÷ 2x = one-fourth.

INTERPRETING STATISTICAL DATA GRAPHS, CHARTS AND TABLES

EXAMINATION SECTION

TEST 1

DIRECTIONS: Each question or incomplete statement is followed by several suggested answers or completions. Select the one that BEST answers the question or completes the statement. *PRINT THE LETTER OF THE CORRECT ANSWER IN THE SPACE AT THE RIGHT.*

Questions 1-9.

DIRECTIONS: Questions 1 through 9 are to be answered SOLELY on the basis of the CLEANERS' WORK PROGRAM given below and the explanatory note.

CLEANERS' WORK PROGRAM

Jobs To Be Done	Monday	Tuesday	Wednesday	Thursday	Friday	Saturday
Sweep floors	X	X	X	X	X	X
Dust furniture	X	X	X	X	X	X
Dust off walls		X		X		
Cleaning lighting fixtures			X			
Wash window sills						X
Clean doors					X	
Empty wastebaskets	X	X	X	X	X	X
Polish hardware		X				
Wash tile	X					
Sweep elevators		X		X		X
Wax chairs			X			
Wax floors					X	
Wax desks				X		
Mop floors	X				X	
Clean cuspidors	X	X	X	X	X	X

EXPLANATORY NOTE: X indicates the day on which the job is to be done.

1. The number of jobs which are scheduled to be done six days a week is 1.____
   - A. 3
   - B. 4
   - C. 5
   - D. 6

2. A job which is scheduled to be done EXACTLY twice a week is 2.____
   - A. cleaning doors
   - B. dusting walls
   - C. sweeping elevators
   - D. emptying wastebaskets

3. Of the following, the BEST reason for giving a cleaner a detailed work program is to 3.____

   A. enable him to improve his skill
   B. aid him to do the most work possible
   C. spread the necessary work over the week as evenly as possible
   D. help him to remember the day of the week

4. The TOTAL number of different jobs which are scheduled for the period shown is 4.____

   A. 6 B. 15 C. 20 D. 35

5. The number of different jobs to be done on Wednesday is 5.____

   A. 8 B. 7 C. 6 D. 5

6. Floors are washed 6.____

   A. every day
   B. Wednesday *only*
   C. Mondays and Fridays
   D. three times a week

7. The SMALLEST number of different jobs to be done on any day is 7.____

   A. 5 B. 6 C. 7 D. 8

8. The one of the following jobs which is done LEAST often is 8.____

   A. dusting furniture
   B. sweeping elevators
   C. waxing floors
   D. dusting walls

9. One job which is NOT scheduled to be done on Fridays is 9.____

   A. mopping floors
   B. cleaning doors
   C. sweeping elevators
   D. waxing floors

KEY (CORRECT ANSWERS)

1. B
2. B
3. C
4. B
5. C
6. C
7. B
8. C
9. C

TEST 2

Questions 1-7.

DIRECTIONS: Questions 1 through 7 are to be answered SOLELY on the basis of the TABULATION OF TURNSTILE READINGS shown below and to the notes given beneath the tabulation.

TABULATION OF TURNSTILE READINGS

Turnstile Number	Turnstile Readings At					
	5:30 AM	6:00 AM	7:00 AM	8:00 AM	-9:00 AM	10:00 AM
1	38921	38931	39064	39435	39704	39843
2	67463	67486	67592	68148	68917	69058
3	65387	65408	65611	66414	67324	67461
4	22538	22542	22631	23061	23613	23720

NOTE: 1. Turnstiles are operated by fares costing 90 cents each.
2. The subway entrance at which these turnstiles are located is open, with a railroad clerk on duty, from 5:30 A.M. to 10:00 A.M.

1. The number of passengers using Turnstile No. 3 from 7:00 A.M. to 8:00 A.M. was 1.____

   A. 203 B. 803 C. 910 D. 1197

2. The turnstile used by the MOST passengers from 8:00 A.M. to 9:00 A.M. was No. 2.____

   A. 1 B. 2 C. 3 D. 4

3. The number of passengers using Turnstile No. 4 in the FIRST half hour was 3.____

   A. 4 B. 10 C. 21 D. 23

4. The TOTAL number of passengers using Turnstile No. 2 from opening to closing was 4.____

   A. 922 B. 1182 C. 1595 D. 2074

5. The MOST used turnstile from opening to closing was No. 5.____

   A. 1 B. 2 C. 3 D. 4

6. From 8:00 A.M. to 9:00 A.M., the railroad clerk sold exactly 1000 fares, while the turnstile readings for the four turnstiles show that a total of 2500 passengers passed through them in the same period. 6.____
   The number of passengers who purchased fares was MOST probably

   A. *less* than 1000
   B. *exactly* 1000
   C. *between* 1000 and 1500
   D. *exactly* 2500

7. The cash taken in for the 1000 fares in Question 6 above was 7.____

   A. $15 B. $100 C. $900 D. $1500

KEY (CORRECT ANSWERS)

1. B
2. C
3. A
4. C
5. C
6. A
7. C

TEST 3

Questions 1-8.

DIRECTIONS: Questions 1 through 8 are to be answered SOLELY on the basis of the charts given below and notes.

RECORD OF TRAFFIC COUNT

LINE: T2 STATION: CROSSROADS TRACK: S.B. EXPRESS

Date: April 24

Head Car No.	Time	No. of Pass. in 3rd Car Arr.	Lv.	Total Cars
6410	8:36	190	120	10
5704	8:33	190	120	10
6683	8:36	200	120	10
5996	8:39	210	130	10
1803	8:42	210	120	10
499	8:45	230	120	10
6341	8:48	230	110	10
887	8:51	240	100	10
6014	8:54	250	100	10
512	8:57	250	80	10

NOTE : 1. Crossroads Station is in midtown and is a heavily used transfer point.

2. Past traffic counts taken at Crossroads Station show that the distribution of passengers in the various cars of the train is approximately as follows:

POSITION OF CAR IN TRAIN	1	2	3	4	5	6	7	8	9	10
Arriving car load in percent of most heavily loaded arriving car	60	80	100	100	100	100	90	90	80	70
Leaving car load in percent of most heavily loaded leaving car	70	100	100	80	60	50	80	100	100	100

1. The number of passengers in the first car of the first train shown in the tabulation when it arrived at Crossroads Station was about 1.____

A. 133 B. 126 C. 114 D. 108

2. The number of passengers in the last car of the 851 interval when it left Crossroads Station was about 2.____

A. 190 B. 120 C. 100 D. 80

3. The TOTAL number of passengers on all ten cars of the 836 interval when it arrived at Crossroads Station was about 3.____

A. 2000 B. 1740 C. 1620 D. 1400

4. The total number of passengers on all ten cars of the 830 interval when it left Crossroads Station was about 4.____

A. 1400 B. 1080 C. 1044 D. 1008

5. Considering that Crossroads Station is a heavily used transfer point, the total number of passengers alighting from the 3rd cars of all of the ten trains shown MOST probably was 5.____

A. 980
B. between 980 and 1080
C. 1080
D. more than 1080

6. The total number of passengers by which the arriving load on all ten cars of the 845 interval exceeded the leaving load on that interval was 6.____

A. 2001 B. 1080 C. 1008 D. 993

7. Of the following conclusions that may be drawn from examination of the car numbers in the first column, the one MOST likely to be correct is that 7.____

A. at least 6000 cars are assigned to this service
B. alternate trains have different destinations
C. any car can be coupled in a train with any other car
D. more than one type of car equipment is in use

8. From examination of the number of passengers arriving and leaving on successive trains, it is PROBABLY valid to conclude that 8.____

A. many of the passengers exiting at Crossroads Station must report to work by 9:00 A.M.
B. most people using line T2 southbound get off at or before Crossroads Station
C. people riding past Crossroads Station generally report to work later than 9:00 M.
D. line T2 is operating at practically its maximum capacity

KEY (CORRECT ANSWERS)

1. C
2. C
3. B
4. D
5. D
6. D
7. D
8. A

TEST 4

Questions 1-7.

DIRECTIONS: Questions 1 through 7 are to be answered SOLELY on the basis of the ROSE LINE TIMETABLE given below. Assume that all operations proceed without delay unless otherwise stated in any question.

TIMETABLE - ROSE LINE
DAILY TRAIN SCHEDULE

David Pl.	Alice St.	15 Av.	St. Helena Av.	Howard Terminal		St. Helena Av.	15 Av.	Alice St.	David Pl.	
Lv.	Lv.	Lv.	Lv.	Arr.	Lv.	Lv.	Lv.	Lv.	Arr.	Lv.
7:15	7:30	7:44	7:58	8:13	8:17	8:32	8:46	9:00	9:15	9:25
7:23	7:38	7:52	8:06	8:21	8:25	8:40	8:54	9:08	9:23	9:35
P7:31	7:46	8:00	8:14	8:29	8:33	8:48	9:02	9:16	9:31	L
7:39	7:54	8:08	8:22	8:37	8:41	8:56	9:10	9:24	9:39	9:45
P7:45	8:00	8:14	8:28	8:43	8:47	9:02	9:16	9:30	9:45	9:55
7:51	8:06	8:20	8:34	8:49	8:53	9:08	9:22	9:36	9:51	L
		P8:23	8:37	8:52	8:56	9:11	L9:25			
7:57	8:12	8:26	8:40	8:55	8:59	9:14	9:28	9:42	9:57	10:05
P8:03	8:18	8:32	8:46	9:01	9:05	9:20	9:34	9:48	10:03	L
8:09	8:24	8:38	8:52	9:07	9:11	9:26	9:40	9:54	10:09	10:20
8:17	8:32	8:46	9:00	9:15	9:19	9:34	L9:48			
P8:25	8:40	8:54	9:08	9:23	9:27	9:42	9:56	10:10	10:25	10:35
8:33	8:48	9:02	9:16	9:31	9:35	9:50	10:04	10:18	10:33	L
P8:41	8:56	9:10	9:24	9:39	9:43	9:58	10:12	10:26	10:41	10:50
8:49	9:04	9:18	9:32	9:47	9:51	10:06	10:20	10:34	10:49	L
8:57	9:12	9:26	9:40	9:55	9:59	10:14	10:28	10:42	10:57	11:05
P9:05	9:20	9:34	9:48	10:03	10:07	10:22	10:36	10:50	11:05	L
9:15	9:30	9:44	9:58	10:13	10:17	10:32	10:46	11:00	11:15	11:20

NOTES: 1. P indicates that a train is placed in service at the station where the letter P appears.
2. L indicates that a train is taken out of service at the station where the letter L appears.

1. The running time between St. Helena Ave. and Howard Terminal is ______ minutes. 1.____

A. 15 B. 29 C. 33 D. 45

2. A passenger arrives at Howard Terminal at 8:52. The EARLIEST time that he could arrive at David Pl. is 2.____

   A. 9:25 B. 9:42 C. 9:57 D. 10:05

3. The length of time spent by each train at Howard Terminal is ______ minutes. 3.____

   A. 6 B. 4 C. 10 D. 8

4. The total roundtrip time including relay time at Howard Terminal for the train leaving David Pl. at 8:49 is ______ minutes. 4.____

   A. 60 B. 200 C. 120 D. 100

5. The number of trains placed in service at David Pl. between 7:39 and 8:33 is 5.____

   A. 1 B. 2 C. 3 D. 4

6. The TOTAL number of trains taken out of service at David Pl. between 9:45 and 10:25 is 6.____

   A. 1 B. 2 C. 3 D. 4

7. The MINIMUM headway leaving David Pl. is ______ minutes. 7.____

   A. 8 B. 3 C. 10 D. 6

KEY (CORRECT ANSWERS)

1. A
2. C
3. B
4. C
5. C
6. B
7. D

TEST 5

Questions 1-7.

DIRECTIONS: Questions 1 through 7 are to be answered SOLELY on the basis of the sample schedule shown below. Assume that all operations proceed as scheduled unless otherwise stated in the question.

ROGER DEPOT

ROUTE: A-4 Logan Blvd.
WEEKDAY SCHEDULE NO. BB-3
EFFECTIVE 1/1/15

HEADWAYS		RUNNING TIME		
From Jane St. and from Carol St.		From Jane St. and from Carol St.		
12:00 Mid.	-		11:00 P.M.	7:00 A.M
4:30 A.M.	20 Min.		7:00 A.M.	11:00 P.M
7:00 A.M.	15 Min.			
10:00 A.M.	4 Min.	Jane St.	- Min.	-Min.
3:00 P.M.	8 Min.	George St.	8 Min.	10 Min.
7:00 P.M.	5 Min.	Nick St.	7 Min.	9 Min.
12:00 Mid.	15 Min.	Burt St.	9 Min.	12 Min.
		Erica St.	6 Min.	9 Min.
		Sam St.	4 Min.	7 Min.
		Len St.	11 Min.	13 Min.
		Tom St.	5 Min.	7 Min.
		Carol St.	10 Min.	11 Min.
			60 Min.	78 Min.

SOUTHBOUND BUSES LEAVE FROM JANE ST.
NORTHBOUND BUSES LEAVE FROM CAROL ST.

1. The bus leaving Jane Street at 6:15 A.M. should arrive at Carol Street at ______ A.M. 1.____

   A. 7:15 B. 7:18 C. 7:24 D. 7:33

2. The bus leaving Jane Street at 6:30 A.M. should arrive at Len Street at ______ A.M. 2.____

   A. 7:07 B. 7:15 C. 7:20 D. 7:38

3. The buses leaving Jane Street at 6:30 A.M. and 6:45 A.M. should arrive at Carol Street ______ minutes apart. 3.____

   A. 15 B. 17 C. 19 D. 21

4. The southbound bus leaving Nick Street at 6:45 A.M. should arrive at Tom Street at _______ M. 4.____

A. 7:20 B. 7:27 C. 7:38 D. 7:48

5. If the southbound bus leaving Jane Street at 6:30 A.M. is delayed for 6 minutes at Burt Street, it will then arrive at Tom Street at _______ A.M. 5.____

A. 7:24 B. 7:36 C. 7:43 D. 7:46

6. If the layover time at Carol Street is 5 minutes, a bus leaving Jane Street at 5:45 A.M. should return to Jane Street at _______ A.M. 6.____

A. 7:50 B. 7:55 C. 8:07 D. 8:12

7. If the distance from Jane Street to Carol Street is 14 miles, then the bus leaving Jane Street at 7:00 A.M. should be traveling at an average speed that is CLOSEST to _______ mph. 7.____

A. 10.8 B. 12.2 C. 13 D. 14

KEY (CORRECT ANSWERS)

1. B
2. C
3. D
4. B
5. B
6. C
7. A

TEST 6

Questions 1-8.

DIRECTIONS: Questions 1 through 8 are to be answered SOLELY on the basis of the schedule given below.

DAILY TRAIN SCHEDULE
Q EXPRESS

SOUTHBOUND							NORTHBOUND			
Bar St.		Love St.	Tom St.	Ann St.	Bell Ave.		Ann St.	Tom St.	Love St.	Bar St.
Arr.	Lv.	Lv.	Lv.	Lv.	Arr.	Lv.	Lv.	Lv.	Lv.	Arr.
7:10	7:20	7:26	7:34	7:44	7:48	7:54	7:58	8:08	8:16	8:22
P	7:30	7:36	7:44	7:54	7:58	8:04	8:08	8:18	8:26	8:32
7:30	7:40	7:46	7:54	8:04	8:08	8:14	8:18	8:28	8:36	8:42
P	7:48	7:54	8:02	8:12	8:16	8:22	8:26	8:36	8:44	8:50
7:50	7:56	8:02	8:10	8:20	8:24	8:30	8:34	8:44	8:52	9:00
P	8:04	8:10	8:18	8:28	8:32	8:38	8:42	8:52	9:00	9:08
8:04	8:10	8:16	8:24	8:34	8:38	8:44	8:48	8:58	9:06	9:14
8:10	8:16	8:22	8:30	8:40	8:44	8:50	8:54	9:04	9:12	9:20
P	8:22	8:28	8:36	8:46	8:50	8:56	9:00	9:10	9:18	9:26
8:16	8:26	8:32	8:42	8:50	8:54	9:00	9:04	9:14	9:22	9: 30L
8:22	8:30	8:36	8:46	8:54	8:58	9:04	9:08	9:18	9:26	9:34
8:32	8:36	8:42	8:52	9:00	9:04	9:10	9:14	9:24	9:32	9:40
P	8:42	8:48	8:58	9:06	9: 10	9:16	9:20	9:30	9:38	9:46

1. A passenger arrives at Bar Street at 8:12. He takes the next train leaving Bar Street to Bell Ave. If he stays on this train, he will return to Bar Street at 1.____

   A. 8:16 B. 9:14 C. 9:20 D. 9:26

2. For the time period shown on the schedule, the number of trains placed in service at Bar Street which make one trip and then lay up is 2.____

   A. 0 B. 1 C. 2 D. 3

3. The SMALLEST headway for trains leaving Bar Street for the period shown on the schedule is_______ minutes. 3.____

   A. 2 B. 4 C. 6 D. 8

4. A motorman leaves Bar Street with the 8:04 train. The amount of time required to travel to Bell Avenue and back to Bar Street is _______ minutes. 4.____

   A. 56 B. 64 C. 68 D. 70

5. The train that leaves Bar Street at 7:20 will, on the next trip, leave Bar Street at 5.____

A. 7:30 B. 8:16 C. 8:22 D. 8:30

6. The TOTAL number of trains stopping at Tom Street between 8:22 and 8:38 is 6.____

A. 2 B. 3 C. 4 D. 5

7. The southbound train leaving Ann Street at 8:54 should be followed by the train which left Bar Street at 7.____

A. 8:22 B. 8:36 C. 8:46 D. 9:00

8. The length of time the southbound train which left Love Street at 7:46 spends at Bell Avenue is _______ minutes. 8.____

A. 6 B. 8 C. 10 D. 12

KEY (CORRECT ANSWERS)

1. C	5. B
2. A	6. D
3. B	7. B
4. B	8. A

TEST 7

Questions 1-8.

DIRECTIONS: Questions 1 through 8 are to be answered SOLELY on the basis of the WEEKDAY TRAIN SCHEDULE - DUMONT LINE.

WEEKDAY TRAIN SCHEDULE - DUMONT LINE

	EASTBOUND					WESTBOUND		
Train No.	Harvard Square Lv.	Pleasure Plaza Lv.	Hard-ing St. Lv.	Magic Mall		Harding Street Lv .	Pleasure Plaza Lv.	Harvard Square Arr.
				Arr .	Lv.			
69	7:48	7: 51	7:56	8:00	8:06	8:10	8:15	8:18
70	7:54	7:57	8:02	8:06	8:12	8:16	8:21	8:24
71	8:00	8:03	8:08	8:12	8:18	8:22	8:27	8:30
72	8:04	8:07	8:13	8:17	8:22	8:26	8:31	8:34
73	8:08	8:11	8:17	8:21	8:26	8:30	8:35	8:38
74	8:12	8:15	8:20	8:24	8:30	8:34	8:39	8:42
75	8:16	8:19	8:24	8:28	8:34	8:38	8:43	8:46
69	8:20	8:23	8:28	8:32	8:38	8:42	8:47	8:50
70	8:26	8:29	8:34	8:38	8:44	8:48	8:53	8:56

1. Train #70 is scheduled to leave Pleasure Plaza on its second westbound trip to Harvard Square at 1.____

   A. 7:57 B. 8:21 C. 8:29 D. 8:53

2. The time it should take Train #74 to go from Harvard Square to Magic Mall is ______ minutes. 2.____

   A. 8 B. 12 C. 18 D. 30

3. As shown on this schedule, the number of trains arriving at Magic Mall and standing there for less than 6 minutes before leaving is 3.____

   A. none B. 2 C. 7 D. 9

4. The number of trains shown on the schedule having different train numbers is 4.____

   A. 6 B. 7 C. 8 D. 9

5. Going towards Harvard Square, Train #71 is scheduled to leave Pleasure Plaza at 5.____

   A. 8:03 B. 8:18 C. 8:27 D. 8:30

6. Passengers boarding at Harding Street and wishing to get to Harvard Square by 8:45 would have to board a train which is scheduled to leave Magic Mall no later than 6.____

   A. 8:26 B. 8:30 C. 8:34 D. 8:38

7. Train #73 should leave Harding Street on its eastbound trip_______ minutes after leaving Harvard Square. 7._____

A. 7 B. 8 C. 9 D. 10

8. Due to door trouble, Train #72 (eastbound) is turned at Harding Street when it was scheduled to leave, and this operation takes 5 minutes. 8._____
Since the running time for the return trip back to Harvard Square is the same time as that for the eastbound trip, it should arrive back at Harvard Square at

A. 8:22 B. 8:28 C. 8:31 D. 8:39

KEY (CORRECT ANSWERS)

1. D
2. B
3. B
4. B
5. C
6. B
7. C
8. B

TEST 8

Questions 1-6.

DIRECTIONS: Questions 1 through 6 are to be answered SOLELY on the basis of the chart given below.

Name of Officer	Date Assignment Made	Days Assigned	Tour of Duty	Facility	Station
Clark, Joseph	11/18	Tues.-Sat .	7 A.M.-3 P.M.	Seamans Tunnel	Post A
Feins, Arthur	10/22	Fri.-Tues.	11 P.M.-7 M.	Lyons Central Bridge	Lane 2
Fine , Howard	10/15	Mon.-Fri.	7 A.M.-3 P.M.	Nimmons Street Bridge	Lane 2
Finia, Maria	11/25	Sat. -Wed.	3 P.M.-11 P.M.	Nimmons Street Bridge	Lane 4
Rivera, Juan	11/25	Wed. -Sun.	3 P.M.-11 P.M.	Seamans Tunnel	Post A
Sussman, Joan	10/15	Sun.-Thur.	11 P.M.-7 M.	Livingston Tunnel	Post B
West, Michael	10/22	Fri.-Tues.	3 P.M.-11 P.M.	Lyons Central Bridge	Lane 2
KEY TO ABBREVIATIONS:		Mon. - Monday Tues . - Tuesday Wed. - Wednesday Thur. - Thursday		Fri. - Friday Sat. - Saturday Sun . - Sunday	

1. Which one of the following officers had an assignment to the Nimmons Street Bridge dated 11/25? 1.____

   A. Joseph Clark
   B. Howard Fine
   C. Maria Finia
   D. Juan Rivera

2. Which of the officers was assigned to a Lane 2 station on October 15? 2.____

   A. Arthur Feins
   B. Howard Fine
   C. Joan Sussman
   D. Michael West

3. The officers whose assignments were made AFTER November 19 are 3.____

   A. Juan Rivera and Michael West
   B. Maria Finia and Juan Rivera
   C. Joseph Clark, Maria Finia, and Juan Rivera
   D. Arthur Feins, Howard Fine, Joan Sussman, and Michael West

4. The number of officers assigned to work ONLY during P.M. hours is 4.____

   A. 2 B. 3 C. 4 D. 5

5. How many officers are NOT assigned to work on Sundays? 5.____

   A. 1 B. 2 C. 3 D. 4

6. According to the above chart, two officers were assigned to the same facility and station during the same days of the week, but they worked different tours of duty. This station is NOT covered by either of these officers on these days from 6.____

   A. 7 A.M. to 3 P.M.
   B. 7 P.M. to 3 A.M.
   C. 3 P.M. to 11 P.M.
   D. 11 P.M. to 7 A.M.

KEY (CORRECT ANSWERS)

1. C
2. B
3. B
4. B
5. B
6. A

INTERPRETING STATISTICAL DATA GRAPHS, CHARTS AND TABLES

EXAMINATION SECTION TEST 1

DIRECTIONS: Each question or incomplete statement is followed by several suggested answers or completions. Select the one that BEST answers the question or completes the statement. *PRINT THE LETTER OF THE CORRECT ANSWER IN THE SPACE AT THE RIGHT.*

Questions 1-9.

DIRECTIONS: Questions 1 through 9 are to be answered SOLELY on the basis of the bus timetable shown below. Assume layover time at Prince St. and Duke St. is negligible.

TIMETABLE - REGENT PARKWAY LINE - WEEKDAYS

	EASTBOUND					WESTBOUND		
Bus No.	King St. Lv.	Prince St. Lv.	Duke St. Lv.	Queen St. Arr.	Queen St. Lv.	Duke St. Lv.	Prince St. Lv.	King St. Arr.
20	7:15	7:20	7:30	7:45	7:50	8:05	8:15	8:20
21	7:25	7:30	7:40	7:55	8:00	8:15	8:25	8:30
22	7:35	7:40	7:50	8:05	8:10	8:25	8:35	8:40
23	7:45	7:50	8:00	8:15	8:20	8:35	8:45	8:50
24	7:55	8:00	8:10	8:25	8:30	8:45	8:55	9:00
25	8:05	8:10	8:20	8:35	8:40	8:55	9:05	9:10
26	8:10	8:15	8:25	8:40	8:43	8:58	9:08	9:13
27	8:15	8:20	8:30	8:45	8:48	9:03	9:13	9:18
28	8:20	8:25	8:35	8:50	8:53	9:08	9:18	9:23
20	8:30	8:35	8:45	9:00	9:05	9:20	9:30	9:35
21	8:40	8:45	8:55	9:10	9:15	9:30	9:40	9:45
22	8:50	8:55	9:05	9:20	9:25	9:40	9: 50	9:55

1. The TOTAL running time (omit layover) for one roundtrip from King St. to Queen St. and back again is _______ minutes. 1.____

   A. 70 B. 65 C. 60 D. 30

2. The LEAST time that any bus stops over at Queen St. is _______ minutes. 2.____

   A. 3 B. 5 C. 10 D. 15

3. The time required for a bus to make the Eastbound run from King St. to Queen St. is _______ minutes. 3.____

   A. 65   B. 60   C. 35   D. 30

4. The TOTAL number of different buses shown in the timetable is 4.____

   A. 8   B. 9   C. 10   D. 12

5. The timetable shows that the total number of buses which make two roundtrips is 5.____

   A. 1   B. 2   C. 3   D. 4

6. A person reaching Duke St. at 8:28 to leave on a Westbound bus will have to wait _______ minutes. 6.____

   A. 2   B. 5   C. 7   D. 10

7. The SHORTEST running time between any two bus stops is _______ minutes. 7.____

   A. 3   B. 5   C. 10   D. 15

8. The bus which arrives at King St. three minutes after the preceding bus is Bus No. 8.____

   A. 20   B. 22   C. 26   D. 28

9. Bus No. 21 is scheduled to start its second roundtrip from King St. at 9.____

   A. 9:45   B. 8:40   C. 8:30   D. 7:25

KEY (CORRECT ANSWERS)

1. C
2. A
3. D
4. B
5. C
6. C
7. B
8. C
9. B

TEST 2

Questions 1-10.

DIRECTIONS: Questions 1 through 10 are to be answered SOLELY on the basis of the DAILY TRAIN SCHEDULE given below.

DAILY TRAIN SCHEDULE *RR* LOCAL											
SOUTHBOUND							NORTHBOUND				
Wall St.		Ann St.	Deer St.	Bay St.	Ellen St.		Bay St.	Deer St.	Ann St.	Wall St.
Arr .	Lv.	Lv.	Lv.	Lv.	Arr .	Lv.	Lv.	Lv.	Lv.	Arr.
6:00	6:12	6:20	6:24	6:30	6:32	6:42	6:44	6:50	6:54	7:02L
6:10	6:22	6:30	6:34	6:40	6:42	6:52	6:54	7:00	7:04	7:12
6:20	6:32	6:40	6:44	6:50	6:52	7:02	7:04	7:10	7:14	7:22
6:30	6:42	6:50	6:54	7:00	7:02	7:12	7:14	7:20	7:24	7:32L
6:40	6:52	7:00	7:04	7:10	7:12	7:22	7:24	7:30	7:34	7:42
P	7:02	7:10	7:14	7:20	7:22	7:32	7:34	7:40	7:44	7:52
P	7:10	7:18	7:22	7:28	7:30	7:40	7:42	7:48	7:52	8:00
7:12	7:18	7:26	7:30	7:36	7:38	7:48	7:50	7:56	8:00	8:08
7:22	7:26	7:34	7:38	7:44	7:46	7:56	7:58	8:04	8:08	8:16
P	7:34	7:42	7:46	7:52	7:54	8:04	8:06	8:12	8:16	8:24
P	7:40	7:48	7:52	7:58	8:00	8:10	8:12	8:18	8:22	8:30
7:42	7:46	7:54	7:58	8:04	8:06L					

1. Between 7:00 and 7:38, the TOTAL number of trains placed in service at Wall St. is 1.____

   A. 1 B. 2 C. 3 D. 4

2. The number of trains which are taken out of service at Wall St. between 7:10 and 8:06 is 2.____

   A. 0 B. 1 C. 2 D. 3

3. Between 7:30 and 7:54, the length of time spent by each train at Ellen St. is ________ minutes. 3.____

   A. 2 B. 6 C. 8 D. 10

4. The headway leaving Ann St. in the southbound direction after the time of 7:42 is ________ minutes. 4.____

   A. 4 B. 6 C. 8 D. 10

5. The TOTAL number of roundtrips between Wall St.. and Ellen St. during the period shown on the schedule is 5.____

   A. 9 B. 10 C. 11 D. 12

6. The train arriving at Ellen St. at 7:38 is followed by the train which leaves Wall St. at 6.____

A. 7:22 B. 7:26 C. 7:36 D. 7:46

7. The MINIMUM headway shown on this schedule for a train leaving Deer St. is _______ minutes. 7.____

A. 4 B. 6 C. 8 D. 10

8. The TOTAL number of trains stopping at Bay St. between 6:45 and 7:25 is 8.____

A. 4 B. 6 C. 8 D. 10

9. The LONGEST travel time for a train elapses between _______ St. and _______ St. 9.____

A. Wall; Ann
B. Ann; Deer
C. Deer; Bay
D. Bay; Ellen

10. A train which arrives at Wall St. at 7:12 will next time arrive at Wall St. at 10.____

A. 7:22 B. 8:08 C. 8:16 D. 8:24

KEY (CORRECT ANSWERS)

1. C
2. B
3. D
4. B
5. C
6. B
7. B
8. C
9. A
10. B

TEST 3

Questions 1-13.

DIRECTIONS: Questions 1 through 13 are to be answered SOLELY on the basis of the PORTERS' WORK PROGRAMS shown below and the accompanying explanatory note.

CLEANERS' WORK PROGRAMS AT HUSTLE ST. STATION

Jobs To Be Done	#1 Tour of Duty 8 A.M. to 4 P.M.							#2 Tour of Duty 4 P.M. to Midnight						
	M	T	W	T	F	S	A	M	T	W	T	F	S	S
Sweep entrance & street stairways	X	X	X	X	X	X	X	X	X	X	X	X	X	X
Sweep interior stairways	X	X	X	X	X	X	X	X	X	X	X	X	X	X
Scrap interior stairways								X	X	X	X	X	X	X
Empty vending machine receptacles	X		X		X		X		X		X		X	
Clean toilets & porters' room		X		X		X		X		X		X		X
Disinfect toilets		X				X								
Dust benches, handrails, booths, etc.	X											X		
Clean columns										X				
Clean signs				X				X					X	
Clean booths														X
Bag paper	X		X		X		X		X		X		X	
Scrap station & toilets	X	X	X	X	X	X	X							

Explanatory Note: *X* indicates the day on which the job is to be done. For example: Clean columns on #2 tour on Wednesdays only.

1. The TOTAL number of jobs to be done as shown on this schedule is 1.____
   A. 5 B. 6 C. 12 D. 14

2. On Tour #1, the GREATEST number of jobs is scheduled to be done on 2.____
   A. Monday B. Wednesday C. Friday D. Saturday

3. On Tour #2, the GREATEST number of jobs is scheduled to be done on 3.____
   A. Monday B. Wednesday C. Friday D. Saturday

4. The number of jobs which are scheduled to be done twice every day is 4.____
   A. 1 B. 2 C. 3 D. 4

5. The number of jobs which are scheduled to be done once every day is 5.____
   A. 2 B. 3 C. 4 D. 5

6. The job which is scheduled to be done once on EACH tour during the week is 6.____

A. clean signs
B. clean booths
C. dust benches
D. disinfect toilets

7. The job which is scheduled to be done once during the week is 7.____

A. clean signs
B. clean booths
C. dust benches
D. disinfect toilets

8. The number of jobs which are scheduled to be done only once during the week is 8.____

A. 1 B. 2 C. 3 D. 4

9. During the week, the porter on Tour #1 is scheduled to clean toilets 9.____

A. twice B. 3 times C. 4 times D. 7 times

10. Trash receptacles under chewing gum machines are to be emptied 10.____

A. 3 times a week
B. 4 times a week
C. every day
D. twice a day

11. The number of different jobs scheduled to be done on Thursdays is 11.____

A. 5 B. 6 C. 8 D. 10

12. Handrails should be dusted on Tour #2 on the same day as 12.____

A. vending machines receptacles are emptied
B. paper is bagged
C. toilets are cleaned
D. the station is scrapped

13. You can infer, after reading all the Jobs To Be Done, that *scrap interior stairway* means 13.____

A. sweep them
B. disinfect them
C. clean the handrails
D. pick up litter from them

KEY (CORRECT ANSWERS)

1. C
2. A
3. D
4. B
5. D
6. C
7. B
8. B
9. B
10. C
11. C
12. C
13. D

TEST 4

Questions 1-10.

DIRECTIONS: Questions 1 through 10 are to be answered SOLELY on the basis of the portion of a timetable shown below.

TIMETABLE - *HH* LINE - WEEKDAYS

NORTHBOUND						SOUTHBOUND			
Train No.	Hall St. Lv.	Ann St. Lv.	Best St. Lv.	Knob Ave. Arr .	Knob Ave. Lv.	Best St. Lv.	Ann St. Lv.	Hall St. Arr .	Hall St. Lv.
88	7:35	7:50	8:05	8:15	8:20	8:30	8:45	9:00	9:05
89	7:50	8:05	8:20	8:30	8:35	8:45	9:00	9:15	9:20
90	8:05	8:20	8:35	8:45	8:50	9:00	9:15	9:30	9:35
91	8:20	8:35	8:50	9:00	9:05	9:15	9:30	9:45	9:50
92	8:30	8:45	9:00	9:10	9:15	9:25	9:40	9:55	10:00
93	8:40	8:55	9:10	9:20	9:25	9:35	9:50	10:05	10:10
94	8:50	9:05	9:20	9:30	9:35	9:45	10:00	10:15	10:20
95	9:00	9:15	9:30	9:40	9:45	9:55	10:10	10:25	10:30
88	9:05	9:20	9:35	9:45	9:50	10:00	10:15	10:30	LU*
96	9:10	9:25	9:40	9:50	9:55	10:05	10:20	10:35	10:40
97	9:15	9:30	9:45	9:55	10:00	10:10	10:25	10:40	LU*
89	9:20	9:35	9:50	10:00	10:05	10:15	10:30	10:45	10:50

NOTE: LU* means that the train is taken out of passenger service at the location where LU appears. Assume that the arrival times at Ann St. and Best St. are the same as the leaving times.

1. The TOTAL number of different train numbers listed in the portion of the timetable shown is 1._____

   A. 9 B. 10 C. 11 D. 12

2. For Train No. 95, the average of the running times from Hall St. to Ann St., from Ann St. to Best St., and from Best St. to Knob Ave. is about ________ minutes. 2._____

   A. 12 B. 13 C. 14 D. 15

3. A passenger leaving Hall St. on the 7:50 train is going to Knob Ave. to take care of some business. 3._____
   If his business takes a total of one hour, he can be back at Hall St. by about

   A. 8:50 B. 9:20 C. 10:15 D. 10:40

4. A passenger reaching Ann St. at 9:17 to leave on a northbound train would expect to arrive at Knob Ave. at 4._____

   A. 9:35 B. 9:45 C. 9:50 D. 10:15

5. The TOTAL number of trains for which two complete round-trips are shown in the timetable is 5.____

A. 4 B. 3 C. 2 D. 1

6. A person reaching Best St. at 9:03 to board a southbound train would have to wait until 6.____

A. 9:05 B. 9:10 C. 9:15 D. 9:20

7. The length of time required for any train to make the northbound run from Hall St. to Knob Ave. is _______ minutes. 7.____

A. 40 B. 45 C. 50 D. 85

8. The length of time that trains are scheduled to remain at Hall St. is _______ minutes. 8.____

A. *always* 5
B. *always* 10
C. *always* 15
D. *either* 5 or 10

9. From the entries in the timetable, you can infer that the location near which there is MOST likely to be a subway yard to store trains is 9.____

A. Ann St. B. Best St. C. Knob Ave. D. Hall St.

10. For Train No. 91, the TOTAL length of time, including the 5-minute layover at Knob Ave., required for one roundtrip from Hall St. to Knob Ave. and return is _______ minutes. 10.____

A. 80 B. 85 C. 90 D. 120

KEY (CORRECT ANSWERS)

1. B	6. C
2. B	7. A
3. C	8. A
4. B	9. D
5. C	10. B

TEST 5

Questions 1-14.

DIRECTIONS: Questions 1 through 14 are to be answered SOLELY on the basis of the portion of the EMPLOYEES' TIME SHEET shown on the following page. When answering these items, refer to this time sheet and the accompanying explanatory note. It contains all of the essential information required to determine the amount earned by each employee, and enough computations are made to show you the method for filling in the blank spaces in the timesheet. For your own convenience, you are advised to compute and fill in the blank spaces in your test before answering any of these items. Then answer each of the items in the usual way.

EMPLOYEES' TIME SHEET												
										Time		
	Pay No.	Name	Hourly Rate	Time Reporting Date	AM	PM	Time Leaving Date	AM	PM	Actually Worked	Overtime Credit	Pay due
REGULAR TIME	41	King	$15.60	2-2-	7:00		2-2-		3:00	8 hrs.	X	62.
	39	Lee	14.40	2-2-		11:00	2-3-	7:00			X	
	85	Mark	16.20	2-3-	7:00		2-3-		3:00		X	
	64	Narr	15.00	2-3-		3:00	2-3-		11:00		X	
	75	Orr	14.40	2-4-		3:00	2-4-		11:00		X	
	29	Peer	16.20	2-5-	7:00		2-5-		3:00		X	
	36	Ray	15.60	2-5-		11:00	2-6-	7:00			X	
	45	Sill	15.60	2-6-	7:00		2-6-		3:00		X	
	91	Tone	14.40	2-6-		3:00	2-6-		11:00		X	
OVERTIME	41	King	$15.60	2-2-		3:00	2-2-		5:00	2 hrs.	3 hrs.	23.
	39	Lee	14.40	2-3-	7:00		2-3-	8:20				
	85	Mark	16.20	2-3-		3:00	2-3-		3:40			
	64	Narr	15.00	2-3-		11:00	2-3-		11:40			
	75	Orr	14.40	2-4-		11:00	2-5-	12:20				
	29	Peer	16.20	2-5-		3:00	2-5-		3:20			
	36	Ray	15.60	2-6-	7:00		2-6-	8:00				
	45	Sill	15.60	2-6-		3:00	2-6-		4:20			
	91	Tone	14.40	2-6-		11: 00	2-7-	12:40				
NOTE: All overtime credit is at the rate of time and one-half.												

1. On February 3, Mark should be credited for both regular time and overtime with a total of_______ hours_______ minutes. 1.____

   A. 8; 40 B. 9; 0 C. 9; 20 D. 9; 40

2. The individuals listed on the time sheet are designated by 2.____

   A. pay numbers B. hourly rates C. overtime rates D. dates

3. The difference between the maximum and the minimum hourly rates of pay as shown in the table is 3.____

   A. 60¢ B. $1.20 C. $1.80 D. $2.40

4. The man earning the LARGEST amount for overtime (of the following) was 4.____

A. Sill B. Tone C. Lee D. Orr

5. The man who earned $16.20 for base pay was 5.____

A. Narr B. Mark C. Orr D. Ray

6. The number of men entitled to less than 9 hours pay was 6.____

A. 1 B. 2 C. 3 D. 4

7. Of the following, the man who put in the LEAST overtime was 7.____

A. Lee B. King C. Narr D. Orr

8. The two men earning the SMALLEST amount for overtime were 8.____

A. Narr and Peer
B. Narr and Mark
C. Mark and Ray
D. Ray and Peer

9. The table shows that more men were needed for overtime at ______ than at ______. 9.____

A. 7:00 A.M.; 3:00 P.M.
B. 7:00 A.M.; 11:00 P.M.
C. 11:00 P.M.; 3:00 A.M.
D. 11:00 P.M.; 7:00 A.M.

10. If Peer's overtime was due to the late arrival of his relief who is paid at the hourly rate of $14.40, then the extra cost to the Transit Authority was 10.____

A. 90¢ B. $1.10 C. $1.80 D. $3.30

11. On February 3, the man earning the LARGEST amount for overtime was 11.____

A. Lee B. Mark C. Narr D. Orr

12. On February 6, Sill's pay for overtime was ______ of his total earnings. 12.____

A. 15% B. 20% C. 25% D. 30%

13. On February 6, Ray received a total pay of 13.____

A. $124.80 B. $132.60 C. $140.40 D. $148.20

14. On February 3, the total cost for overtime was 14.____

A. $31.20 B. $43.80 C. $45.00 D. $60.00

KEY (CORRECT ANSWERS)

1. B	6. A	11. A
2. A	7. C	12. B
3. C	8. A	13. D
4. B	9. D	14. D
5. B	10. D	

TEST 6

Questions 1-11.

DIRECTIONS: Questions 1 through 11 are to be answered SOLELY on the basis of the time-table shown below and the accompanying notes.

TIMETABLE - CROSSTOWN LINE LOCALS
WEEKDAYS WITHOUT SATURDAY

NORTHBOUND				SOUTHBOUND							
Cable St.	Fail St.	Duke Pl.	Gain St.	Lack Ave.		Gain St.	Duke Pl.		Fail St.	Cable St.	
Lv.	Lv.	Lv.	Lv.	Arr.	Lv.	Lv.	Arr.	Lv.	Lv.	Arr.	Lv.
P7:20	7:35	7:48	7:58	8:12	8:18	8:32	-	8:42	8:55	9:10	9:20
-	-	P7:52	8:02	8:16	8:22	8:36	8:46	8:52	-	-	-
7:28	7:43	7:56	8:06	8:20	8:26	8:40	-	8:50	9:03	9:18	9:28
	-	8:00	8:10	8:24	8:30	8:44	8:54	9:00	-	-	-
7:36	7:51	8:04	8:14	8:28	8:34	8:48	-	8:58	9:11	9:26	9:38
-	-	8:08	8:18	8:32	8:38	8:52	9:02	9:10	-	-	-
P7:44	7:59	8:12	8:22	8:36	8:42	8:56	-	9:06	9:19	9:34	L
-	-	P8:16	8:26	8:40	8:46	9:00	9:10	9:20		-	-
7:52	8:07	8:20	8:30	8:44	8:50	9:04	-	9:14	9:27	9:42	9:48
-	-	8:23	X	8:47	8:53	9:07	9:17	L	-	-	-
7:58	8:13	8:26	8:36	8:50	8:56	9:10	-	9:20	9:33	9:48	9:58
-	-	8:29	8:39	8:53	8:59	9:13	9:23	9:30	-	-	-
P8:04	8:19	8:32	8:42	8:56	9:02	9:16	-	9:26	9:39	9:54	L
-	-	8:35	8:45	8:59	9:05	9:19	9:29	9:40	-	-	-
8:10	8:25	8:38	8:48	9:02	9:08	9:22	-	9:32	9:45	10:00	10:08
-	-	P8:41	8:51	9:05	9:11	9:25	9:35	L	-	-	-
8:16	8:31	8:44	8:54	9:08	9:14	9:28	-	9:38	9:51	10:06	10:18
-	-	8:47	8:57	9:11	9:17	9:31	9:41	9:50	-	-	-
8:22	8:37	8:50	9:00	9:14	9:20	9:34	-	9:44	9:57	10:12	L
-	-	8:52	9:02	9:16	9:22	9:36	9:46	L	-	-	-
8:26	8:41	8:54	9:04	9:18	9:24	9:38	-	9:48	10:01	10:16	10:28
-	-	P8:56	9:06	9:20	9:26	9:40	9:50	10:00	-	-	-
P8:30	8:45	8:58	9:08	9: 22	9: 28	9:42	-	9:52	10:05	10:20	L

NOTES:
1. P denotes that a train is placed in passenger service where the letter P appears.
2. L denotes that a train is taken out of passenger service where the letter L appears.

1. The TOTAL number of scheduled roundtrips between Cable St. and Lack Ave. during the period shown is 1._____

   A. 8 B. 12 C. 19 D. 23

2. The scheduled running time between Cable St. and Lack Ave. is ____ minutes. 2.____

A. 48 B. 52 C. 58 D. 90

3. The number of trains which are laid up after making one roundtrip from Cable St. is 3.____

A. 1 B. 2 C. 3 D. 4

4. The number of trains which are laid up after making one roundtrip from Duke Pl. is 4.____

A. 1 B. 2 C. 3 D. 4

5. Before 9:00, there is a train leaving Lack Ave. every ____ minutes. 5.____

A. 2 or 3 B. 3 C. 4 D. 3or4

6. After 9:00, there is a train leaving Lack Ave. every ________ minutes. 6.____

A. 2 B. 2 or 3 C. 3 D. 3or4

7. The train which is put in at Duke St. at 7:52 is scheduled to lay up after its second roundtrip at 7.____

A. 8:52 B. 9:44 C. 9:46 D. 9:48

8. The timetable indicates that a number of storage tracks or a yard is located near 8.____

A. Gain St. B. Fail St. C. Duke Pl. D. Lack Ave.

9. If a passenger arrives on the Gain St. Station at 9:00, he can expect to get to Cable St. at 9.____

A. 9:48 B. 9:42 C. 9:34 D. 9:27

10. The number marked *X* which has been omitted from the leaving column at Gain St. is 10.____

A. 8:32 B. 8:33 C. 8:34 D. 8:35

11. Assuming that the headway leaving Cable St. southbound does not change after 10:28, the train which is scheduled to leave NEAREST Noon is scheduled to leave Cable St. at 11.____

A. 11:46 B. 11:48 C. 11:58 D. 12:08

KEY (CORRECT ANSWERS)

1. B
2. B
3. C
4. A
5. D
6. B
7. C
8. C
9. B
10. B

11. C

TEST 7

Questions 1-8.

DIRECTIONS: Questions 1 through 8 are to be answered SOLELY on the basis of the portion of the ARRIVAL TIMETABLE for Bay St. local station of the subway shown below. This table shows the times when trains are scheduled to arrive at Bay St. Station. Refer to this timetable, and consider only the period of time covered by the table when answering these questions.

ARRIVAL TIMETABLE

SOUTHBOUND				NORTHBOUND			
Col. 1	Col. 2	Col. 3	Col. 4	Col. 5	Col. 6	Col. 7	Col. 8
Mon. PM to Fri. AM	Fri. PM to Sat. AM	Sat. PM to Sun. AM	Sun. PM to Mon. AM	Mon. PM to Fri. AM	Fri. PM to Sat. AM	Sat. PM to Sun. AM	Sun. PM to Mon. AM
11:42	11:42	11:42	11:44	11:44	11:44	11:25	11:44
11:54	11:52	11:52	11:54	11:54	11:54	11:33	11:54
12:06	12:02	12:02	12:06	12:04	12:04	11:41	12:04
12:18	12:12	12:12	12:18	12:14	12:14	11:49	12:14
12:30	12:22	12:22	12:30	.12:24	12:24	11:57	12:24
12:42	12:34	12:32	12:42	12:34	12:34	12:05	12:34
12:54	12:46	12:42	12:54	12:46	12:44	12:15	12:46
1:09	12:58	12:52	1:09	12:58	12:54	12:25	12:58
1:24	1:13	1:02	1:24	1:10	1:04	12:35	1:10
1:44	1:28	1:14	1:44	1:22	1:14	12:45	1:22
2:04	1:41	1:26	2:04	1:34	1:24	12:55	1:34
2:24	1:56	1:38	2:24	1:46	1:34	1:05	1:46

1. Two columns which show exactly the SAME arrival time for every train are Columns _______ and _______ . 1.____

   A. 1; 3 B. 2; 4 C. 5; 8 D. 6; 7

2. The number of nights per week to which Column 1 applies is 2.____

   A. 5 B. 4 C. 3 D. 1

3. The TOTAL number of northbound trains scheduled to arrive at Bay St. Station from 12:45 A.M. to 1:15 A.M. on Tuesday is 3.____

   A. 5 B. 3 C. 2 D. 1

4. The TOTAL number of all trains scheduled to arrive at this station between 11:45 P.M. Friday and 1:30 A.M. Saturday is 4.____

   A. 9 B. 10 C. 19 D. 21

5. A northbound train is due at this station at 12:34 A.M. every day of the week EXCEPT 5.____

   A. Friday B. Saturday C. Sunday D. Monday

6. A passenger who wants to get a northbound train anytime after 11:59 P.M. on Wednesday can tell from the timetable that the MAXIMUM length of time he must wait for the next train if he just misses one is _______ minutes. 6.____

   A. 15 B. 12 C. 10 D. 8

7. The TOTAL time elapsed from the first to the last train of Column 6 is_______ hours _______ minutes. 7.____

   A. 2; 10 B. 2; 30 C. 1; 50 D. 1; 10

8. If a passenger who wishes to board a southbound train arrives on Bay St. platform at Midnight on Saturday, he can expect to board a train at 8.____

   A. 12:06 B. 12:05 C. 12:04 D. 12:02

KEY (CORRECT ANSWERS)

1. C
2. B
3. B
4. C
5. C
6. B
7. C
8. D

PUBLIC TRANSPORTATION TO POINTS OF INTEREST IN MANHATTAN AND THE BRONX

MANHATTAN

Battery Park – State Street & Battery Place
- (a) R Local to Whitehall St./South Ferry Station
- (b) W Local to Whitehall St./South Ferry Station
- (c) No. 1 Broadway/7th Ave. Local to South Ferry Station

Central Park Mall – 72nd Street
- (a) No. 1, B or C Local to 72nd St. Station; walk east to center of park
- (b) Nos. 2/3 7th Ave. Express to 72nd St. Station; walk east to center of park
- (c) Buses: M66 or M72

Central Park Zoo & Children's Zoo – 64th Street off 5th Avenue
- (a) R/W Local to 5th Ave. Station
- (b) N Express to 5th Ave. Station
- (c) No. 6 Lexington Ave. Local to 68th St. Station; walk west to park

Cloisters – Fort Tryon Park
- (a) A train to 190th St. Station

Damrosch Park – 62nd Street & Amsterdam Avenue
- (a) No. 1 Broadway/7th Ave. Local to 66th St./Lincoln Center Station
- (b) Buses: M5, M7, M10, M11, M66 and M104 all within one block of park

Delacorte Theater ("Shakespeare in the Park") – Central Park, West Drive, near 81st St.
- (a) B/C Local to 81st St./Museum of Natural History Station; enter park at 81st St.
- (b) No. 1 Broadway/7th Ave. Local to 79th St. Station; walk north to 81st St.; east to park
- (c) Bus, M10 Central Park West to 81st St.; M79

East River Park – East River at Grand Street
- (a) B Local/D Express to Grand St. Station
- (b) J/M Express to Essex St. Station; Bus 14A/14D to river
- (c) F train to Delancey St. Station; Bus 14A/14D to river

Fort Tryon Park

Follow directions to Cloisters

Icahn Stadium – Randall's Island, East River & 125th Street
- (a) No. 4, 5, or 6 Lexington Ave. Express or Local to 125th St. Station; M35 bus to Randall's Island

Inwood Hill Park – 211th Street & Seaman Avenue
(a) A train to 207th St. Station

Jumel Mansion – 162nd Street & Jumel Terrace, Washington Heights
(a) C train to 163rd St. Station
(b) No. 1 Broadway/7th Ave. Local to 157th St. Station

Lasker Memorial Rink – Central Park, 110th St. opposite Lenox Avenue
(a) 2/3 Express to 110th St. Station

Metropolitan Museum of Art – 82nd Street & 5th Avenue
(a) No. 4, 5, or 6 Lexington Ave. trains to 86th St. Station

Mount Morris Park – 5th Avenue & 120th Street
(a) No. 4, 5, or 6 Lexington Ave. trains to 125th St. Station
(b) 2/3 Express to 125th St. Station; walk east to park

Museum of Natural History – 79th Street & Central Park West
(a) B Local (weekdays) or C Local to 81st St./Museum of Natural History Station
(b) No. 1 Broadway/7th Ave. Local to 79th St. Station

Sarah D. Roosevelt Park & Golden Age Center – Delancey Street between Chrystie & Forsyth Streets
(a) B/D trains to Grand St. Station
(b) J Express or M Local to Bowery Station

(Alfred E.) Smith Recreation Area – Catherine Street between Madison and South Streets
(a) Bus, M15 to Catherine St.
(b) F train to East Broadway, walk west to park

Ward's Island Recreation Area – Ward's Island
(a) Footbridge from FDR Drive & East 103rd St.

Wollman Memorial Ice Rink – Central Park, west of 64th Street
(a) A/C, B/D, 1/9 trains to 59th St. Station
(b) N/R trains to 5th Ave. Station
(c) B/Q trains to 57th St. Station

Jay Hood Wright Playground & Golden Age Center – Fort Washington Avenue & 173rd St.
(a) A train to 175th St. Station

THE BRONX

Botanical Garden – Bronx Park, 200th Street near Webster Avenue
(a) No. 2 or 5 Express to Pelham Parkway Station
(b) B/D or No. 4 trains to Bedford Park Blvd. Station
(c) Bx26 Bus east from Bedford Park Blvd. Station

Bronx Zoo – Bronx Park, Fordham Road & Southern Boulevard
(a) No. 5 Express to East Tremont Ave./Boston Rd. Station
(b) No. 2 Express to East Tremont Ave./Boston Rd. Station
(c) Bus: Bx9/Bx19 to 183rd/Southern Blvd.; Bx12/Bx22 to Fordham Rd./Southern Blvd.

Claremont Park – East 170th Street & Clay Avenue
(a) D train to 170th St. Station; walk six blocks east

Crotona Park – Fulton Avenue and East 172nd Street
(a) No. 5 Express to 174th St. Station
(b) No. 2 Express to 174th St. Station

(Owen) Dolen Park, Golden Age Center – East Tremont & Westchester Avenues
(a) No. 6 Local to Westchester Square/East Tremont Ave. Station

Orchard Beach & Pelham Bay Park – Bruckner Boulevard & Pelham Parkway
(a) No. 6 Local to Pelham Bay Park, then Bx12 bus City Island/Fordham to Beach

Poe Park – Grand Concourse & Kingsbridge Road
(a) B/D train to Kingsbridge Rd. Station
(b) No. 4 Express to Kingsbridge Rd. Station; walk two blocks east

St. Mary's Park Recreation Center – East 145th Street & St. Ann's Avenue
(a) No. 5 Express to 149th St./3rd Ave. Station
(b) No. 2 Express to 149th St./3rd Ave. Station
(c) No. 6 Express to 143rd/St. Mary's Station

Van Cortlandt Park – Broadway, Jerome Avenue, Van Cortlandt Park East and South, & City Line
(a) No. 1 Local to 242nd St./Van Cortlandt Park Station
(b) No. 4 Express to Woodlawn Station

Wave Hill Center for Environmental Studies – Independence Avenue & 248th Street
(a) A train to 207th St. Station; Bx7 bus to 246th St.
(b) No. 1 Local to 231st St. Station; Bx7 or Bx10 bus to 246th St.